SEARCHING FOR HORNBEAM

A SOCIAL HISTORY

CHRIS HOWKINS
NICK SAMPSON

PUBLISHED BY
CHRIS HOWKINS

COPYRIGHT
© Text and Illustrations Chris Howkins 2000

PUBLISHER
Chris Howkins, 70 Grange Road,
New Haw, Addlestone, Surrey,
KT15 3RH

PRINTED
Unwin Brothers Ltd., The Gresham Press,
Old Woking, Surrey, England.
GU22 9LH

CONDITIONS OF SALE
This book is sold subject to the condition that it shall not, by way of trade or otherwise be lent re-sold, hired out or otherwise circulated in any form of binding or cover other than that in which it is published and without a similar condition including this condition being imposed upon the subsequent purchaser.

ALL RIGHTS RESERVED
No part of this publication may be reproduced, stored in a retrieval system, or transmitted in any form or by any means electronic, mechanical, photocopying, recording or otherwise without the prior permission of the publisher.

ISBN 1 901087 20 4

CONTENTS

INTRODUCTION and ACKNOWLEDGEMENTS 4

WHAT IS A HORNBEAM TREE? 8

THE RANGE OF THE HORNBEAM 10

IS IT A NATIVE? 11

WHAT'S IN A NAME? 12

AND SO TO WORK 13

THE HIGHEST QUALITIES 14

THE COBBLER 17

THE GARDENER 21

THE FUEL MERCHANT 25

THE MILLER 31

THE MUSICIAN 40

THE PLOUGHMAN 46

SPORTS and GAMES 49

THE THRESHER 55

THE TURNER 57

THE WHEELWRIGHT 70

THE WOODSMAN 74

THE WOODWORKER 78

BIBLIOGRAPHY 81

CHECK LIST 83

INDEX 84

INTRODUCTION

Searching for Hornbeam started off as a much smaller study to fill a gap left by *Trees and People*. There was only a page and half of uses on our data base and they were not very inspiring - 'screws' for example. Little did we realise that by exploring such key words would we explore such diverse topics as medieval table manners or the rotation of a cartwheel. Nor did we expect so much fieldwork, up in the top of a windmill one week and down the bottom of a garden in the workshop of a harpsichord maker the next. Apart from being the more rewarding phase of the work it was also essential, as published texts proved either unhelpful or else contradictory. There's no substitute for talking to people who still use the wood nor for seeing them do it. At this stage it would be very satisfying to be able to think the study was 'complete' but only a bat head believes he's the last word on the subject and we know full well that there are questions unanswered. Whereas most people were extremely informative and encouraging there were also those who reputedly use the wood today but who would not co-operate in the slightest. Further information from readers would be appreciated. What we hope is that this study introduces the reader to the *main* uses of the timber and some of the lesser. Obviously such categories as 'turned objects' could be endless - turners used whatever was to hand for such mundane items as egg cups. We have tried to give some indication of when particular uses came into being but closing dates are much more difficult, especially as some craftsmen have to work traditionally where authenticity is demanded, as in restoration work.

One use, presumed to be minor, we have not had any success with whatsoever and that is for steles. We didn't find it on any published list but it is in the Oxford English Dictionary. It quotes Roger Ascham in 1643 reporting *'steles be made of 'diuverse woodes as brasell[1]..hardbeam...etc.'* The O.E.D. gives the familiar inscribed stone slab definition for stele but adds *'occas. loosely, any prepared surface on the face of a building, a rock, etc. covered with an inscription.'* So did Ascham have wooden notice boards in mind?
Another very odd item, where seeing has to be believing, was shown to us in the museum collections at the Royal Botanic Gardens, Kew. It's a

---

[1] Brassell = red dye wood from South America that gave its name to Brazil. Bot. *orig. Caesalipina sappa* but now *C. echinata*

sample of veneer (17 x 14cm), believed to be late 19th century, from the United States. That's an unlikely source and a very unlikely product but there is a note with this item, by a Dr. Asa Gray, which reads: "*The shavings are removed from the trunks by a gigantic planing machine. They can be supplied in America at about the same cost of ordinary wall paper.*"

There are a couple of modern uses missing from this study until results can be evaluated. Apparently, Hornbeam logs have been infected with the mycelium of edible fungi ready for enthusiasts to grow at home, while the Russians are assessing its value for removing uranium from polluted soil.

Although the uses found so far have proved to be very diverse there are some areas where Hornbeam wood might have proved valuable but we have failed to trace evidence, so far. In particular we wondered whether it was used for fitting out early shipping, since pulleys (for rigging ?) get listed. Dr. Ian Friel[2] discussed this with us at length, pointing out that he knew of no references to date. Early records do not specify the woods used except sometimes timbers being ordered in bulk, such as Oak or Spruce. With increasing interest in marine archaeology and the recovery of more material from wrecks, our knowledge is expanding. One tiny item has been found, which we cannot report until the finder's own report has been published.

At all times we've endeavoured to remember that we are trying to reveal the uses of Hornbeam and not to get drawn beyond that: hammer heads for pianos does not lead into a summary of the complete instrument nor millwheels into a study of milling. We've concentrated on the role of Hornbeam whether immediate, as in axles, or by helping to sustain the lives and aspirations of our ancestors, as in table manners. Indeed, it is the people whom we've borne in mind throughout, since this is primarily a social history of the tree.

Many people have been wonderfully supportive with this particular study and we thank them all. In particular, we thank the officers at the Royal Botanic Gardens, Kew, not only for granting access to their

---

[2] authority on the subject; author of *The Good Ship:- Ships, Shipbuilding and Technology in England 1200-1520;* British Museum Press; 1995

library but also for retrieving eighteen items out of their museum collections which we were permitted to examine at will. Most sources are acknowledged but some people gave out information unofficially and asked for their names to be omitted; we thank these in particular as often their knowledge was vital.

The research and early drafts are the combined effort of myself and Nick Sampson but I have to take responsibility for the faults in the final version. C.H.

PUNCTUATION: in the interests of effective communication, especially for readers not familiar with plant names, we have followed our usual practice of adopting the older system of giving capital letters to names in English. This saves confusion where the name begins with an adjective. There is always a problem over tenses when old skills are still practised but on the whole, as this is a social history book, we have used the past tense, with apologies to those craftsmen who are still alive and well. To satisfy political correctness we have used BCE (Before Common Era) for BC and CE (Common Era) for AD.

FOLKLORE: often the lore gives valuable insights into the past uses of our plants but Hornbeam was conspicuous for its absence from our collections. It does feature, unfavourably, in the instructions of a Saxon fertility rite (10th and 11th century texts): *"Then take oil and honey and yeast, and milk of each animal that is on the land, and a piece of each type of tree that grows on the land, except hardbeams, and a piece of each herb known by name, except burdock only...."*[3]

---

[3] see Jolly, Karen; *Popular Religion in Late Saxon England – Elf Charms in Context*; Univ. of N. Carolina Press; 1996

ACKNOWLEDGEMENTS

This study has demanded that much of the material already in print be verified as accurate and to this end a wide diversity of professionals and enthusiasts have shared their knowledge and expertise. They helped to make the background research a fascinating 'treasure hunt' and in particular we should like to express our appreciation to the following:

Amenity usage: Brenda Lewis, Historic Parks and Gardens Officer, Surrey County Council.

Conservation depts.: Stephen Fry, Surrey County Council; Paul Sutton, Epping Forest Council.

Document research: Gillian Edom; Ian Friel; Laura Hastings, Centre for Economic Botany, Royal Botanic Gardens, Kew; Elizabeth Lewis; Hazel Putland; Paul Strike; R. G. Whitehead.

Footwear: Roz Sherris, Sec. Early Dept. Museum of London; Brian Hensman, Information Officer, National Collection of Boots and Shoes, Central Museum, Northampton; Steve Porter, orthotist.

Libraries: Guildhall Library; Royal Botanic Gardens, Kew; St. Bride's Printing Library; Surrey County Library.

Musical instruments: The Dolmetsch family; Rosemary Dawborn; Bill Dow, Curator, Finchcocks Living Museum of Music; Andrew Durand; Penny Hollow, Haslemere Educational Museum; Horniman Museum; David P. Hunt; Brenda Lewis; John Storrs.

Screws etc.: Michael Wright, Curator of Mech. Engin. and colleagues at the Science Museum, London.

Technical information: The Arboricultural Association; Dr. Pat Denne, University of Wales, Bangor; Duncan Lorimer; Stuart Salt.

Windmills: Penny Murray, West Sussex County Council, James Woodward-Nutt, miller, Outwood Mill, Surrey and Shipley Mill, West Sussex; David French, Chairman of the Friends of Shipley Mill.

WHAT IS A HORNBEAM TREE?

Scuffling through the golden dryness of autumn leaves where the louring sun shines down through the all-surrounding trees is a childish delight never to outgrow. When these trees are Hornbeams the eye can run up towering fluted trunks and branches for ninety feet to see the last gold pennants fluttering against the blue. Somewhere up there might be the Hornbeam's own special bird, the Hawfinch, (illus. P.10) but this secretive beauty is notoriously difficult to spot. Sadly relatively few people enjoy walking through the Hornbeams because they either live in the wrong area, or the old woods have been felled, or they mistake the trees for Beeches.

The Hornbeam is one of our least known trees. Classified as *Carpinus betulus* L.,it belongs to the Birch family, Betulaceae, hence its specific name *betulus*. Other British trees in the same family are the Alder and the Hazel but neither of them look like Birch trees to the general viewer. The Hornbeam resembles closely an unrelated tree, the Beech. The leaves are very similar, with the Hornbeam's being slightly coarser, more deeply toothed, and more pointed; the differences appear quite subtle to the inexperienced. In early spring the Hornbeam is easy to spot because maturing specimens burst forth bright green catkins, before the leaves, which make the tree look as though it has burst into leaf ahead of its companions. The Beech meanwhile keeps its buds tightly wrapped, only allowing the pompon clusters of flowers to dangle after the leaves have unfurled.

Under favourable conditions the Hornbeam will rise as a fine forest tree to 30m, the same as the average mature Beech, although the latter sometimes reaches another 10m. The Hornbeam can be found in other guises, growing from coppiced stools or as clipped hedges or as pollards. The woods of ancient pollards can be silent and mysterious on winter days as their great grey boles anchor the fluted boughs embracing the softening mist. These are inaugural places for people who don't yet understand the spirit of the trees.

Scans of actual samples for comparison.
Top – Hornbeam
Right - Beech
Note the Hornbeam leaves are more likely to be pointed and toothed than the Beech.

THE RANGE OF THE HORNBEAM

Many people in Britain are unfamiliar with the Hornbeam because it is more of a Continental tree, extending eastwards from the North Sea even further than the Beech but not as far as the Oak. It shuns the more maritime climate of the fringes of Western Europe because it provides late frosts, to which the Hornbeam is sensitive. Such frosts are not a feature of the more Continental climates. Despite this the tree extends its natural range into the south east of England, particularly Essex, Kent, Surrey and Sussex. Scatterings extend further into England to approximately a line drawn from the Wash to Somerset, with a couple of unexplained outliers, such as in Gwent. Elsewhere it has to be planted and can be found right up to Sunderland. Indeed conservationists have been planting hundreds of them in recent years so future generations will be more familiar with them than we are today, even in the south east.

On the Continent look for it from southern Sweden down to the Pyrénées and eastwards across to Italy, Greece and the Caucasus, fading out in Asia Minor. The Hornbeam of North America is a different species, *Carpinus caroliniana*.

Hawfinch, in alarm stance.

IS IT A NATIVE ?

Since the tree has such distinctive pollen grains and fruits for the archaeologists to recognise there is plenty of evidence that the tree was here during the warmest periods of the interglacials, up to the last Ice Age. Then it retreated with all the other trees but was slow to return afterwards. It waited until the climate had really improved - not returning until some 2,500 years after the Oak. There is still debate as to when exactly it became well established. Part of the problem lies in its distribution being primarily in the south east where there has been little work on pollen analysis from ancient soils and peat bogs. It was here about 8,000 BCE but was very slow to get established so that even by 3,000 BCE it was still uncommon. It is believed to have arrived naturally, especially since it yields nothing edible to cause man to introduce it deliberately. Nevertheless there are some who feel it *was* introduced deliberately, about 3,000 BCE. More certain is the close association with man. If given the chance, it will spread rapidly and man provides that chance when he clears woodland for farming or reduces the overhead shade by coppicing and pollarding. Continental research indicates that during wars, when land was left neglected, the Hornbeam spread over it, and, remained after the wars since it is so resistant to cutting and grazing.

Today, it is noticeable that the Hornbeam will recolonise ground from where Beech has been removed but in early times the Beech was a rarity. Caesar looked for it because it was such an important timber tree to the Romans but he declared sadly that there were no Beeches in Britain. He was wrong but locations were few and isolated. Apart from the Beech there are other trees with which the Hornbeam is associated, such as the Field Maple in north Hertfordshire and then, when the land runs over heavy boulder clay, the Hazel associates with it too. On the lighter soils in parts of East Anglia the Ash grows with the Hornbeam, although to the south of the region, through Essex, it grows with Oak, as it does in south Hertfordshire. It is not even possible to make categoric statements about its place in the order of woodland succession. It is often said that all trees will yield ultimately to the Oak yet in Wormley Wood in Hertfordshire it looks as though the Oak is yielding to the Hornbeam[1].

---

[1] From Allaby, pp. 71-2

WHAT'S IN A NAME ?

ENGLISH NAMES
Ay Beech
Candle Tree
Candlewood
Common Hornbeam
Harber/Harbur
Hardbeam
Hornbeam
Horn Beech
Horn Wood
Horst Beech
Hurst Beech
Husbeech
Ironwood
Lanthorn
White Beech
Wych or Witch Hazel
Yoke Elm

The names given to our plants by our forefathers can often reveal uses and qualities. The names for this tree, not just in English but most N. W. European languages, are no exception. They tend to concentrate upon the hardness and strength of the timber.

Hornbeam is given two etymologies. One has it being derived from the Saxon for 'horny wooded tree', referring to the wood being as hard as horn. The other draws attention to it being used for the beam behind the horns of oxen when yoked for ploughing. As the tree was not found throughout the ploughlands of Saxon England it would seem logical to take the first option as the more likely. Indeed the Oxford English Dictionary gives the very late date of 1568 for the earliest surviving record of 'hornbeam'. Before that it was called Hardbeam and that was the more usual name up until about 1800.

When Linnaeus came to classify and name the plants he chose to call the genus by its ancient Latin name, used by Pliny and Vetruvius, and that was Carpinus. It is suggested by Alcock[4] and repeated by Hulme[5] that this derived from the Celtic *car* for wood and *pin* for head, bringing the thinking back to ox-yokes. However, Miller[6] reports there are no such words in Celtic and in any case the language was not that well known in ancient Rome. He offers, somewhat doubtfully, that it might derive from the *carpentum* or covered carriage used by the ladies of Rome, that was said to be made from this timber, (they are much more likely to have used Beech).

---

[4] Alcock, Randal H.; *Botanical Names for English Readers*; L. Reeve and Co.; 1876.
[5] Hulme, F. Edward, *Wild Fruits of the Country-side*, Hutchinson, 1902, p.115.
[6] Miller, Christy; *The Hornbeam in Britain*; J. of Ecology; Vol.XII; No.1; 1924.

As for the other names on the list, Ay Beech means everlasting and refers, it has been suggested, to the way the trees can retain their dead leaves on the twigs through winter. This refers to hedging and brushwood rather than free-growing trees. However, to call it Ay Beech is a bit nonsensical since the Beech does the same thing and therefore the name is of no use in distinguishing between the two. It is more likely to refer to the longevity of the timber, which is more durable than Beech in many situations.

Candle-tree, Candlewood and Lanthorn (i.e. lantern) all refer to the brightness of the flames when the wood burns. When poles from pollards and coppice stools were cleaned up, the twigs were kept for burning to provide artificial light.

Common Hornbeam, Harber or Harbur, Hardbeam, Hornbeam, Horn Beech, Horn Wood all refer to the horn-hard timber. So does Ironwood but that often shows American influence, even if the word came from Europe originally. The New World does not have *Carpinus betulus* as a native but its own species, *Carpinus americana,* now called *Carpinus caroliniana.* Another species, *Carpinus ostrya-americana* became the 'official' Ironwood or Hop-Hornbeam (now called *Ostrya carpinifolia).*

Horst Beech, Hurst Beech, and Husbeech probably reflect the quick regeneration of this species into any new clearing to make their own woodland or 'hurst'. Horse Beech is probably a corruption of this. Horse can sometimes mean *coarse,* as in horse-play.

White Beech reflects the whiteness of the timber. Wych or Witch come from Saxon words meaning pliant, lively, alive - as when the stools and pollards burst back into life with new stems. These are pliant enough for use by the hoopers in the past.

AND SO TO WORK

Hornbeam's working life centres upon its timber, above all other uses. It was obtained in three ways:- by felling the tree, by taking poles from coppiced stools or by taking poles from pollards. For some intended uses, such as constructing windmills, the whole tree was needed. Most other uses required smaller pieces and so these could be serviced from coppice and pollard material, thereby maintaining the renewable resource.

The management of the coppiced and pollarded trees is poorly recorded. We could not trace figures for the density of planting. For the cropping rotation, Miller[7] cites 8-10 years for pollars but draws attention to a document from 1582 wherein the cycle is specified at 15 years (for Monkswood, Epping Forest). For coppice stools (cut to about eighteen inches from the ground) he cites 10-15 years. It must be remembered that these cycles will vary from place to place and time to time, depending upon the intended use and therefore the size of poles required.

We don't know whether poles were harvested selectively or whether the total growth was cut and if so, how often. Regeneration after cutting is much slower than for some other trees treated in these ways, being only about 3ft/1m a year, so poles of a sizeable diameter could only have been harvested on a relatively long cycle. Much quicker would have been the return on twigs and thin branches, which were in demand as fuel and for lighting. If the growth was cut selectively then both demands could be met in perpetuity but not necessarily with the best material of greatest yield per cut.

THE HIGHEST QUALITIES

From the bread in our mouths to the shoes on our feet, Hornbeam wood has played its part. As a preliminary to understanding such a diverse range of applications some thought needs to be given to the characteristic qualities of the wood. Sadly, most books have only a short entry on the subject and even that is likely to be generalised as superlatives. Thus we can read time and again that Hornbeam is the hardest, heaviest, strongest European timber. Is it true?

When it comes to hardness and heaviness many readers will be under the impression that Box, *Buxus sempervirens*, holds the European record, since it is so dense it will not float. Others may know that the Wild Pear, *Pyrus communis,* must be nearly as dense since that will

---

[7] Miller, Christy; *The Hornbeam in Britain*; J. of Ecology; Vol.XII; No.1; 1924.

barely float. For an interpretation of these claims we are indebted to Dr. Pat Denne of the University of Wales, Bangor. She confirmed that Box does have the densest timber, with a specific gravity of 0.91 compared with 0.70 for the Wild Pear. The Hornbeam comes in parallel with the pear at 0.75. The slight difference is not significant, as there will be a margin of variation between samples from different trees. Dr. Denne drew attention to differing viewpoints: the Hornbeam *is* the densest wood but only in terms of commercial timbers used today. Studies of commercial timbers do not normally include Box or Pear because their uses are too specialised and small-scale. This, of course, disproves that popular notion that these timbers will not float. Their specific gravity is less than that of water and so they *will* float. Admittedly, Box only just manages it, with less than a tenth of the wood above water, and therefore it is not serviceable to man in that capacity. This was put to the test and Box *does* float; we tested it twice! A Hornbeam log, axed in half, floats with the flat axed face just proud of the surface.

Thus claims for it being the hardest are true from a commercial viewpoint. That is an important characteristic for any use where the timber has in some way to withstand impact. One test for this is to drop weights on samples and measure the dents. Obviously the weight, the dropping distance and the wood samples all have to be standardised. Results show that Hornbeam is equal to Beech and both are more resistant than Ash but all three are outstripped by Oak.

Resistance to impact is one way of being 'strongest' while another would be its breaking strain. When the maximum bending strength was tested, and measured in Newtons/mm^2, the results were as per column (a) below. Column (b) shows the results when the stiffness was tested, with the modulus of elasticity being measured again in Newtons/mm^2.

(a)		(b)	
Birch	123	Birch	13,300
Hornbeam	119	Beech	12,600
Beech	118	Hornbeam	11,900
Ash	116	Ash	11,900
Oak	97	Oak	10,100

To find the Birch figuring so highly on the tables may surprise many people, who think of the Birch as being rather a weak tree. Appearances can be so deceptive. Most people's idea of our strongest timber would probably be the Oak but much of that reputation stems from good salesmanship. Craftsmen have always regarded the Hornbeam as the stronger of the two because it will not split. It does not cleave under the woodsman's axe or split under stress when in use, which was exploited for early wooden machinery that had to withstand strain, such as windmills. Oak on the other hand cleaves well and is enjoying a revival in fashionable cleft-oak paling around gardens and horse paddocks. When tested scientifically this was proven true. Hornbeam timber cut lengthways, parallel to the grain, has a strength of 17.7 Newtons/mm^2 whereas Oak registers only 13.7. Similarly, if cut across radially, Hornbeam registers 20.8 Newtons/mm^2 and the Oak only 14.5 and it's similar when cut on the tangent: Hornbeam 31.7 and Oak 20.1 Newtons/mm^2.

(Statistics from Table 1, p.209 of Proceedings of the Royal Society of Edinburgh, 85B, 1984.)

Engineering qualities are provided by the above characteristics – a point offered regularly by the harpsichord makers. Thus Hornbeam was often the engineers' material before cast iron was developed. However, all these strengths make the timber extremely difficult to work and therefore craftsmen have avoided it whenever a serviceable substitute was easier. On the whole it was not used for carpentry although under the power of the lathe it does turn well. Even in today's age of machine tools the Hornbeam is still not popular. It blunts chain saws faster than any other tree and then it produces a lot of wastage when it's being prepared in the sawmills. The machinery there squares up timber from tree trunks that start off more or less circular in section, but the Hornbeam is invariably oval and even that can be deeply fluted, so there's plenty of wastage.

For aesthetics and hygiene whiteness is often a desired quality and Hornbeam was the whitest wood in Britain apart from Holly and Box, until the introduction of the Sycamore, in Tudor times. These other trees do not share the same characteristics and so Hornbeam was reserved for some special uses, until timber from later introductions, such as the Tulip Tree, became available. In the 17th century John

Evelyn[8] was commending Hornbeam for its whiteness to the husbandman, and the same 'fine white' quality was still being highlighted by Johnson[9] as late as 1862. Only the *fresh* wood seems to be white. The older pieces, such as those shown us from the museum collections at Kew, have all darkened to a mid brown, about the colour of Cobnuts. Similarly, the fresh log we were given was white, until we used it for the floatation experiments and then it dried flesh coloured over night. It has remained that colour for three months now.

Hornbeam is avoided for outdoor work since it is so dense it will not absorb preservatives, such as creosote. If left untreated it will decay rapidly when exposed to moisture. Thus it has to be seasoned with care, raised above the damp. It is not one of those timbers that can be left in the corner of the yard for a couple of seasons. It rots. It also 'spalts', not so much in the original sense of splitting and becoming brittle but in the sense of developing blackish patterns that break up the natural pattern of the grain - thought to be due to the presence of fungi. These patterns are often desirable in modern decorative wears, such as bowls, where the turner can exploit them as natural decoration.

******

THE COBBLER

In these days of High Street shops selling ready-to-wear, factory-made, boots and shoes it takes a sizeable step back in time to the days when footwear was hand-made specifically for individual customers. Boots and shoes were built up around wooden *lasts* or models of the customer's feet and these lasts can be found in the published lists of Hornbeam uses.

Ordering footwear beforehand is the *bespoke* system of trading and the earliest known use of this term, according to the Oxford English Dictionary, dates from 1583. However, precision shoe-making is far older than that - look up 'last' and we learn that it's an Anglo-Saxon word, so there is obviously a very long history attached to this. Tracing it is a different matter. Relatively few early items of footwear have

---

[8] Evelyn, John; *Silva or a discourse of Forest trees*; 1662 (5th ed. 1729 used).
[9] Johnson, C.P.; *The Useful Plants of Great Britain*; Hardwicke; 1862.

survived, let alone the tools and lasts used in their making. From the little that is known of such things in the 9th and 10th centuries we can say that footwear was well-made, in the sense that accommodation was provided for the big toe on each foot thereby creating a left and right shoe. There was also the option of wooden soles instead of the more usual leather ones but these do not bring us into contact with Hornbeam since a lighter wood was needed. Similarly, when pattens and raised heels were introduced lighter woods were employed.

It should be pointed out that published lists of Hornbeam uses often prefix lasts with *cobblers*, which is misleading and also, we found out, causes offence! A cobbler, strictly speaking, repairs footwear. It was fashioned originally by a shoe-maker and to the trade guilds this was a crucial difference. Guilds of shoe-makers complained that cobblers were 'repairing' footwear to such a degree that they were in effect making a new pair. This was stealing trade and livelihood from the shoe-makers. Soon they became rivals and the legislation introduced to calm and curb the tensions makes fascinating reading. Neither of these factions took kindly to anything they saw as encroachment from a third party. Just such a threat came from the *cordwainers*. These were workers in leather (everything from leather bottles to horse harness) who took their name originally from Spanish Cordoba leather which was made of goatskin (later horse hide). This became very fashionable for shoes, among the wealthy, in the Middle Ages. Thus the cordwainers were attacked for creaming off the top of the market from the shoe-makers and cobblers. Wooden lasts were central to the lives of all three groups of craftsmen.

In the earlier 20th century the local bootmaker was still a familiar and vital craftsman. From Enstone in Oxfordshire, Monty Abbott remembered his:
"He not only measured feet, he sculpted their every corn and callus, building up small bumps of leather on to the basic last. They was made of beech or hornbeam, took nails easily without splitting, and never warped. Each last was unique, faithful; to its owner - and I mean owner. When you pays for a last to be made then that last is youern. You can keep it in a glass case if you wants, corns and all, or you can cart it off to another bootmaker." [10]

---

[10] Stewart; Sheila; *Lifting the Latch - a Life on the Land*; OUP; 1987; pp.58-9.

That's outside the experience of most people today. Rarely have the personalised lasts been kept and even centres of manufacture, like Northampton, sold off their lasts some years ago at 50p a sack for firewood. There are of course people whose feet cannot be accommodated comfortably or healthily in factory produce and have their footwear made specially. It seemed possible that the traditional ways of working might still survive with an orthotist and indeed this avenue of enquiry produced such a craftsman, complete with a Hornbeam last, dating from before 1900, (illus. p.20). It's still in use (not the same client of course!). It was of two pieces, hinged across the *last-break* in such a way that they make a rigid block to work around yet can be released for removal from the finished boot. This basic last had been built up with cork (as opposed to Abbott's leather) to the exact shape of the foot and over this model the leather is *lasted* down using a pair of *lasters* (which were like pliers) until the pieces are shaped correctly and glued. The leather pieces are nailed to the last while the glue dries and then the nails are removed, the sole added, the hinge released and the last removed.

The Museum collections at Kew contain three lasts, all imported from France by Peal & Co. of Grosvenor Square, London. They came from the Association St. Sauveur, Paris, 48. They are 28cm long and 8cm wide although one is left with a headed protuberance from the toe. In addition there is a last block, awaiting final shaping. They've been date stamped 1881. We know a little about Peal and Co. By 1877 they were at 11 Duke Street as waterproof leather bootmakers where they prospered to the extent of moving to 487 Oxford Street by 1889. Their workshops were at Ealing.[11]

When you'd got your expensive personalised footwear home then they could be kept in shape between wearings with last-like 'trees', which again could be made of Hornbeam.

---

[11] inf. courtesy Museum of London.

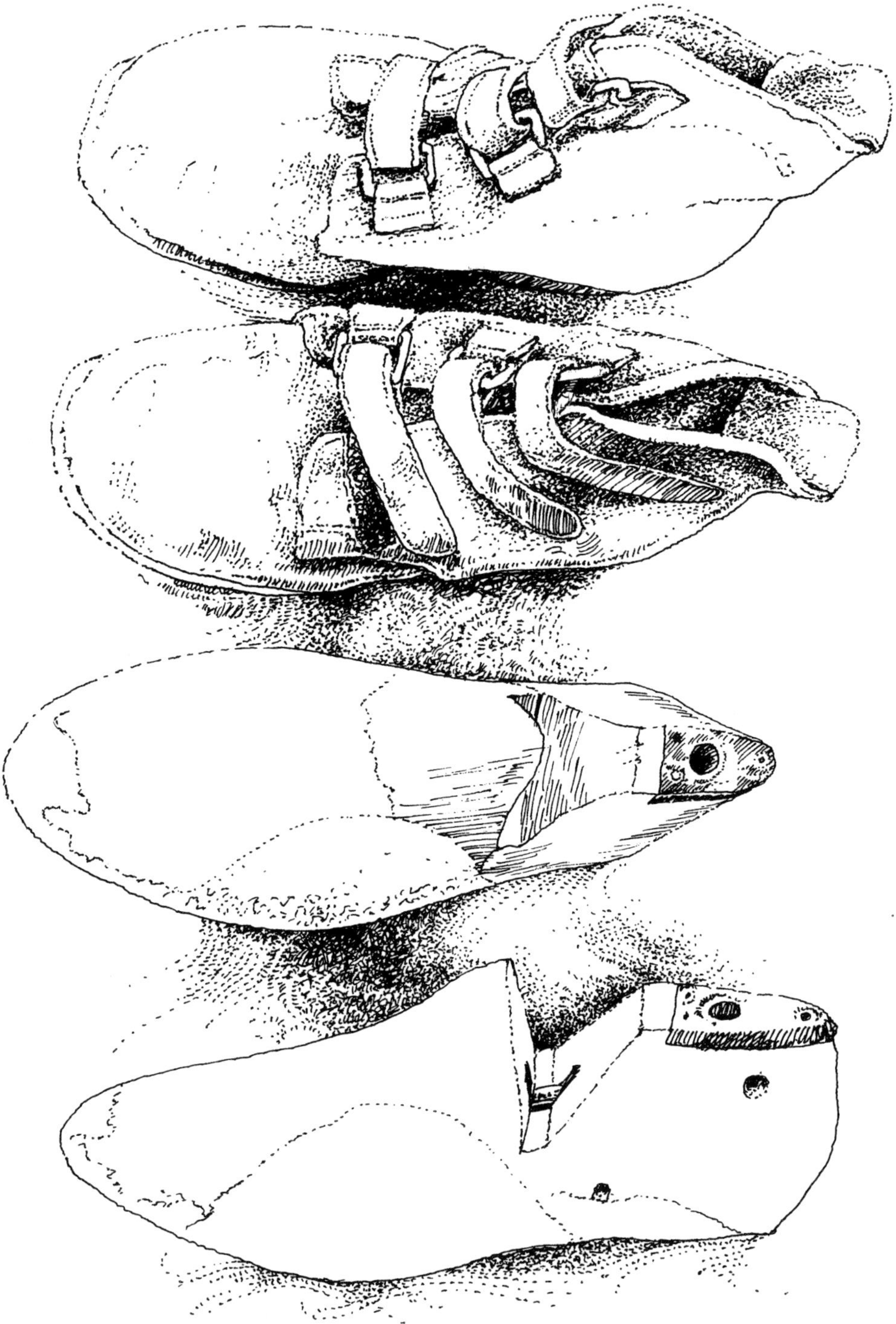

THE GARDENER

A walk in the park, whether in an urban setting, or through a country estate, so often means a walk amid beautiful mature trees. In the early centuries of parks these were places for deer and they were the focal point. By the 17th century the emphasis had shifted considerably from the deer to the value of the landscape and its trees. There were still herds of deer and of course they browsed the trees. From this experience came the knowledge that Hornbeam had an immense power to regenerate, whether from nibbling or deliberate clipping. This made it admirably serviceable when the fashion changed to having part of the park laid out as formal gardens, since the Hornbeam could be trained, pruned and clipped into the desired forms to give permanent structure to the scene. The trees were not simply planted to give structure, as in avenues, but were also trained and pruned into pleached alleys and clipped into hedges for mazes and labyrinths, or were clipped into topiary features.

Continental garden design, especially in France, was ahead of the British and proved to be influential - it provided the first and last impressions as people criss-crossed through France on their European tours. They began to adopt the French ideas so that by the time John Evelyn published his *Silva*, in 1664, he could record, *"That admirable Espalier-hedge in the long middle Walk of Luxemburgh Garden at Paris (than which there is nothing more graceful) is planted of this Tree; and so was that Cradle, or Close-Walk, with that perplext Canopy which lately covered the Seat in his Majesty's garden at Hampton-Court, and as now I hear, they are planted in Perfection at New-Park, the delicious Villa of the noble Earl of Rochester, belonging once to a near Kinsman of mine, who parted with it to King Charles the First of Blessed Memory."*

Evelyn even gives a graphic description of how the formality was achieved on a grand scale– no snipping around with shears – they used scythes: *"These Hedges are Tonsile; but where they are maintained to fifteen or twenty Foot Height (which is very frequent in the Places before mentioned) they are to be cut, and kept in Order with a sithe of four Foot long, anhd very little falcated; this is fixed on a long Sneed, or straight Handle, and does wonderfully experdite the trimming of these and the like Hedges."*

They gave shape and form to the landscape, they guided the pedestrian from viewpoint to viewpoint, they cast valued shade to preserve pale complexions and they shaded many of the sensitive plants being introduced into horticulture. Then fashion changed again to the wild and romantic landscape of which Capability Brown is the best known exponent, but not the first. Out went formality and the Hornbeam with it.

There are exceptions of course. Visit the Belgian gardens of Beloeil, begun in the early 18th century, where, true to its time, you can walk between architectural columns and arches, reflected in still waters. Whereas other gardens had their temples and follies in pale masonry in a green setting, at Beloeil the architecture is contrived from living Hornbeams. The columns have been created by planting two trees very close together and training them, initially, on a wooden framework. Even today, they are not bare-trunked but fully clothed in foliage down to their ankles. Amid lawns and backed by mature broad-leaves, they make a stunning green architectural landscape. In autumn, there's a striking colour contrast when the Hornbeam highlights itself in vibrant gold amid the green lawns. When the backing trees put dark patterns on the winter sky then the Hornbeams are wrapped in warm russet. In spring it's all vivid green again.

The development of smaller personal gardens

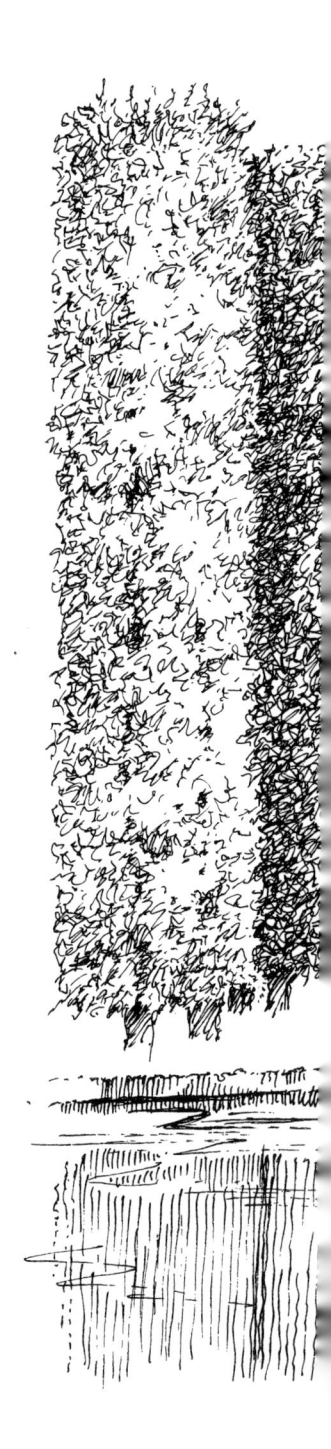

in the 19th century often required hedging but the virtues of the Hornbeam had been largely forgotten. Popular and influential books like William Cobbett's *The English Gardener*, first published in 1829, does not even mention Hornbeam. He describes the virtues of Box instead. Mrs Beeton ignored it too. In *The Beeton Book of Garden Management*, first published in the 1860s, there is much about hedging, but no mention of Hornbeam. Instead, it promotes Holly, Privet, Yew, thorn and conifers. It's with the 20th century that Hornbeam begins to creep back into the press, as an alternative to Beech. Both are recommended for the same reason – when treated as a hedge they do not shed their leaves in winter. They keep them, russet and wrinkled, on the twigs, providing winter colour. Oddly, this was not taken up very widely. Odd, because the fashion for 'winter colour' and making the garden attractive throughout the year was the major contribution to garden history from the 20th century. In the opening years Gertrude Jekyll had been able to refer to winter as *"that quiet time"* when there was little to draw people into the garden. A new enthusiasm for winter flowers and variegated evergreens, and trees with coloured bark became the new fashion. Hornbeam's winter russets were overlooked, perhaps wisely, as gardeners realised that when it came to spring and they wanted everything smart to enhance the bulbs, the hedge would dump a load of dead leaves into the wind! Also, as Christopher Lloyd noted, *"they rustle rather dismally."*[12]

Hornbeam columns
Boloeil

---

[12] Lloyd, Christopher; *The Cottage Garden*; Dorling Kindersley; 1990; p.41.

contribution to garden history through the 20th century was the concept of winter colour. Suddenly the garden had to be attractive throughout the year, without winter being *"that quiet time,"* referred to in Gertrude Jekyll's writings, at the beginning of the century. However, as fashion moved in that direction so there was a contrary flow towards revivalism, especially of the more formal ideas and of French ones in particular. Thus when Lawrence Johnston created his influential Cotswold garden at Hidcote Manor (began 1903) he planted a 'Stilt Garden' of pleached Hornbeams. The notion and design are such as he would have been familiar with from his childhood years spent in France but as so little is known about Johnston that connection should not be asserted as fact. Nevertheless, this was one of the prime gardens, not only for pioneering such concepts as 'garden rooms' but also for influencing some revivalist ideas, such as the formal use of Hornbeam.

In parallel with these developments ran a nostalgia from urban areas for an idealised notion of some 'golden age' in the countryside. Ultimately, by the end of the 19th century, this gave rise to the 'Garden City' designs at places like Bedford Park, Chiswick. The title came from a pioneering work called *Garden Cities of Tomorrow* by Ebenezer Howard, published in 1902. It was not, however, entirely new. It was John Evelyn, again, who had promoted the idea of trees in urban areas, and set out demonstration sites in the West End of London. Some of those trees are said to survive in St. James's Park etc.

Street trees suffer terrible lives – drought, pollution, vandalism and savage pruning. The most tolerant has proved to be the London Plane, to the extent that it is now reckoned to be the commonest street tree in the world. In modern times, early trials were with the Horse Chestnut, prized for its beautiful blooms. However, the necessary pruning resulted too often and too quickly in heart-rot. Cherries provided blossom and autumn colour, and were more tolerant. They too can get heart-rot from hard pruning but, nevertheless, there was considerable enthusiasm for them up until the Second World War. Many new cultivars were being bred to fuel this enthusiasm but it was the blousey double pink 'Kanzan' that became so very popular.

On the whole, attention turned to the smaller trees, such as the golden Laburnums and the Hawthorns, in white or red, single or double, the Mountain Ashes and the Maples. As for large trees, without the virtue of blossom, forms of the Sycamore were popular but attention soon turned to fastigiate trees – those with naturally upward growing branches that wouldn't need the savage pruning. Among the most commonly planted of these was the Lombardy Poplar, *Populus nigra italica*, with its glossy leaves, always shimmering in the breeze, and also Dawyck Beech, *Fagus sylvatica* 'Fastigiata' and a form of the Hornbeam, *Carpinus betulus* 'Fastigiata'. The poplar wasn't new but had come from Italy in 1758 while the Beech was only discovered about 1860 and the Hornbeam in 1885. This Hornbeam can also be found listed as 'Pyramidalis.' It has been much planted in streets and parks, as a rather dark, static feature in the landscape, until it turns gold in the autumn. Other cultivars of the Common Hornbeam, *Carpinus betulus* include:*asplenifolia*, with deeply lobed leaves, *Carpinizza*, with fewer pairs of veins to texture the leaves, *columnaris*, slender spire but only when young, *incisa*, smaller-leaved, *pendula*, pendulous branches, *purpurea*, foliage purplish when young.

******

THE FUEL MERCHANTS

LONDON'S BURNING !

Fuel, whether firewood or charcoal, was the main product from coppicing and pollarding. Hornbeam had the reputation of burning hottest and for longest, so it served well for both household and industrial needs. The greatest market for household fuel from within the Hornbeam's natural range came from London. Although coal was in use from Norman times as an alternative it did not burn as cleanly as wood or charcoal. To give some idea of the quantities involved, the population of London in 1300 has been estimated at 80-100,000 and they would therefore have needed some 100, 000 tons of wood a year for cooking their food.[13]

---

[13] Hammond, P.W.; *Food and Feast in Medieval England*, Wrens Park Publishing; 1998; p.40

Pollard showing it's tendency to produce a mass of poles and twigs of little use except for fuel.

Additionally, there was a high demand for fuel by the food processors and other industries. For example, Hornbeam gets cited[14] as fuel for the brewing industry, for the maltings. Brewing was an important industry in London and the South East, not only because of the density of the population but also because of the concentration of Quakers who took to brewing when their faith curtailed other occupations.

Another industry from Essex was the manufacture of gunpowder that took quantities of charcoal. The favoured source for the Surrey works was Alder (*Alnus glutinosa*) but for Essex Miller records Hornbeam.[15]
In the South East there was an industrial demand for charcoal from the iron industry, since charcoal produces greater heat than either wood or coal. The iron industry, centred in the Weald, was extensive and each furnace required about five tons of charcoal per week, and there's an awful lot of charcoal to the ton! Consequently, most charcoal produced south of the Thames went to the ironmasters. Some did go to London, via centres such as Croydon and Kingston-upon-Thames, but outbidding the ironmasters put the prices high and there was much complaining. It was produced in the great Wealden forest which was primarily of Oak and Hazel; what part, if any, was played by Hornbeam is not known. In some districts the medieval glass industry created a demand for wood fuel which further reduced any surplus for London.

Londoners, therefore, looked to the north side of the Thames for their fuel and much of this was produced from Hornbeam. Places soon became noted for it, particularly Epping Forest, Hainault Forest, Enfield Chase, eastern Hertfordshire and the central Chilterns. Some supplies did come from south of the river, from the North Downs of Kent. Sadly, many woods of old pollards have been destroyed in recent years but a few do still survive and are being preserved. Those in Epping Forest are the best known.

To imagine these woods being worked, picture winter scenes with the leaves off the trees. The collyers/colliers who made the 'small coals' (charcoal) have to be imagined cutting the poles down to some four feet in length and stacking them into the prevailing wind to dry out, ready

---

[14] Miller, Christie; *The Hornbeam in Britain*; J. of Ecology; Vol.XII; No.1; 1924.
[15] See Howkins, Chris.; *Trees, Herbs and Charcoal Burners*.

for a speedy charring. The more they made the more they earned. Ideally, all the poles were best if they were about the same thickness to ensure an evenness of charring in the kiln, so thick poles would be split. The actual charring was summer work. Firewood was cut also through the bare months and stockpiled.

Working Hornbeams in Epping Forest, in the 19th century, as shown in a terracotta panel in the head of the rear doorway to Lopping Hall, Loughton, Essex. See also title page.

The working of the woodland resources in these ways was a vital aspect of the feudal economy and, as far as we know, very successful. However, when this system began to decline and communal land began to pass into private ownership, things changed. They had to, since the resources passed into private hands along with the land - unless provision was made for its continued exploitation. The concept of 'commoners' rights' developed new significance from then on and these were often written into tenancy agreements or the rights were bought up by the landowners. Sometimes the rights were swapped for portions of less desirable land, which are often recorded as 'poors' allotments'.

Thus great areas of forest, such as Epping Forest and Hainault in Essex, shrank dramatically, by thousands of acres. There, however, the people of the Loughton area rebelled and took seventeen of the local landlords to court in order to defend their right. The case ran for sixteen years.Crucially, that halted forest enclosure and destruction throughout the country as anxious landowners awaited the outcome. That story is here paraphrased from that by J. H. Wilks.[16]

The people of the Loughton area had rights allowing the lopping of the Hornbeams for fuel each year from 11th November (St. Martin's Day) till 23rd April (St. George's Day). This was conditional upon the first lopping beginning at midnight of the 10th - an important event in the local social calendar with bonfire and refreshment at Staples Hill prior to midnight. Then they lopped for a couple of hours to stake their claims. One of the landlords called Maitland, who was also their rector, tried to break this pattern. He set up his own party for them, hoping to get them too drunk to stake those claims! He failed. One chap and his two sons slipped off to lop but when they returned to the party the infuriated rector promptly denied his parishioners access to his lands. This led in 1866, to John Willingale, a local fuel merchant, and his two sons, lopping some of Maitland's trees so he prosecuted them for trespass. The court found in favour of Maitland and imprisoned the Willingales, one of whom died of pneumonia in prison. There was a local outcry and people raised a thousand pounds to help John Willingale finance a lawsuit on behalf of them all, with the help of the Commons Society, to win back their rights and prevent further loss of forest. Maitland fought back by trying to ensure Willingale couldn't get employment. When that failed he tried bribing him with £500 to leave the district. That failed too. The case went to court but after four years Willingale died. At least he'd given the poor another four years of rights and more importantly he'd frightened other landowners in the country from proceeding with their own deforestations until the outcome of the case was known. That took sixteen years and cost over £200,000 (think what that would be today!). Part of that cost went as compensation to the poor who had lost their fuel. The rights of people of Loughton were bought for £7,000 but they took only £1,000, towards their costs, and spent the rest on a community centre. Built in 1884, this

---

[16] Wilks, J.H.; *Trees of the British Isles, in History and Legend*; Frederick Muller; 1972; pp.179-180.

still stands today, in the
centre of Loughton,[17] and is one of the finest monuments
to those who worked the fuel rights. The illustration shows the High
Road frontage. Abutting the right hand end, but here edited out, is the
rather gaunt and church-like hall itself. Is this the only building in the
country to commemorate a way of life centred upon a tree?

---

[17] corner of Station Road and High Road (inf. Epping Forest Council).

Part of a well-known anonymous poem about firewood informs us:

> *Beechwood fires burn bright and clear,*
> *Hornbeam blazes too,*
> *If the logs are kept a year,*
> *To season through and through.*

Blaze they did indeed. This is the wood that burns with the brightest flames, providing artificial light by which to practise cottage crafts etc., hence such names as Candlewood or Candle tree, Lanthorn or Lantern. Thus even the twigs were likely to have been sold on. Some of the 'rubbish' was sold as firelighters, called *pimps* in some regions.

******

THE MILLER

THE BREAD IN OUR MOUTHS

Today we can buy a wide range of cereal products from all around the world, without any sense of wonder. It is difficult to appreciate the fears of our ancestors who were so dependent upon the weather. Extremes, whether drought or inundation, destroyed many a harvest and filled minds with foreboding for every harvest. Malnutrition and starvation were constant killers for centuries. For so much of that time there was the added terror that it was the will of God, as a punishment for sins that, on Judgement Day, would bring perpetual damnation. Oh what joyous Harvest Suppers they must have celebrated after really good harvests, such as those of 1730-33. What desperate prayers must have been raised in bad years, like the famine years of 1597 and 1757, and the horror of two successive punishing years of crop failure in 1673 and 1674.

Even when a good harvest had been garnered successfully into rick and granary and barn the fears were not over. Sometimes the grain could not be milled, however great the need. Watermills were rendered useless if their races dried up during droughts or be in such spate from storms that it was unsafe for them to operate. Periods of complete calm brought windmills to a standstill, just as strong winds can make them dangerous or impossible to work. Inclement weather had to be sat out. Seeking outside help was not always legal. Villagers might be restricted by the lord of the manor to use only the mill on his manor and not take trade/wealth/power to his neighbour and certainly not to undermine this system by using a hand quern at home. Thus the reliance upon the daily loaf was fraught with hazard. Artists and early photographers depicting whole communities, young and old, happily heaving corn stooks up on to the wains in glorious sunshine, give little idea of their grim determination fuelled by fear.

For many communities Hornbeam trees have assisted in the provision of that daily loaf. Yokes of its timber harnessed oxen to the plough. It made the threshing floors. It was used probably for flail heads and possibly the central support of post mills and it's still used for the cogs in both windmills and water mills.

MILLING

At some time after flailing and winnowing the grain had to be ground into bread flour. Small amounts could sometimes be ground by hand but most was ground by machine - by using either wind or water power. The watermill was developed at an earlier date than the windmill.

WATERMILLS

Readers will be familiar with the rustic riverside watermill, with its great wheel parallel to a side wall, rotating with the force of the current. What is less well known is what happens inside. The machinery has two prime objectives. One is to turn the power from the vertical wheel through ninety degrees to drive the millstones horizontally. The second is to increase the rotations of the millstones beyond those of the outside wheel.

Thus a watermill is essentially a series of wheels and cogs powered by running water. As the water drives the paddles of the great outer wheel so another wheel, on the same axle, is turned inside the mill. This inner wheel (the *pit* or *pitch* wheel) has cogs instead of paddles and is linked to a smaller horizontal *wallower* wheel above it. That way the drive is

Watermill and castle, Skenfrith, Gwent.

rotated through ninety degrees. This is linked to a bigger wheel, the *spur* wheel, and that to the *spur nut* and that is what drives the millstones. Variations in the sizes of the wheels and the numbers of cogs on each, creates the gearing to ensure the millstones rotate far faster than the paddle wheel outside. For example, if the paddle wheel rotates nine times per minute so the millstones can be geared to rotate 270 times per minute.

Until the development of cast iron in the 18th century all watermill machinery since at least Saxon times, had been made entirely from wood: the axles, the wheels, the cogs, the lot, were all wooden. The timberwork had to withstand the stresses and strains, and these were only as constant as the flow of the water. Accelerations caused major problems, not least to the teeth of the cog-wheels that had to take the increased forces. Thus watermills were made of a variety of timbers. The paddles were of Elm, the pit wheel and its cogs, down in the wet, were of Oak, while Beech could be used in the upper dry areas and cogs up there were of such timbers as Beech, Pear, Apple, Oak, and Hornbeam.

All these constructions and their timbers were treated with care since the whole community's staple food depended upon the mill. For it to break down was serious. Even so, there was the inevitable wear and tear on the wheels but at least controlling water flow helped to maintain an even pressure. Thus when we stand on a mill dam admiring the mill pond we are looking at the first line of defence of one the community's most precious assets. Here, water in spate could be trapped and released at a steady rate.

Inside the mill the cogs in the wheels had to be of a timber that was not only hard wearing but would wear evenly as they continually 'licked' one against the other. The main danger was that one of the cogs should break, as described by Walter Rose:

"Sometimes a faulty cog in one or other of the wheels would break, and before the miller had time to run and turn off the water the wheel had turned round several times and each time the gap came round the impetus caused by the missing cog would cause the next to strike so hard that several more would be broken. In that way a dozen or more would break by the failure of a single cog.[18]*"*

When such a failure brought the whole mill to a standstill all available craftsmen were likely to be called upon to service it as soon as possible. How they must have muttered about the Hornbeam's resistance to the will of their tools! Not only was a single cog quite a large item of subtle tapers but it had to marry absolutely exactly with the cogs in the neighbouring wheel, so when in motion they 'licked' together. In other words, the degree of wear in the cogs of the other wheel had to be taken into account, to ensure that the pressure was always even. Anything

---

[18] Rose, Walter; *The Village Carpenter*; CUP; 1937; p.106.

more, or less, could be disastrous. At the end of the job the millwrights listened to the licking sound of cog against cog to judge the perfection of their achievement. Any imperfection had to be corrected there and then, rather than leave it to 'wear in' because it wouldn't. The fault got worse!

The cogs look deceptively simple. Each cog is a wedge large enough to penetrate the mortices right through the thickness of the felloe or rim of the wheel, towards its centre, and project beyond. Through this projection some millwrights drove a nail to ensure the wedge could never work itself out. Returning to the thick end, proud above the felloe, this was shouldered to restrict the depth to which it could be driven through the felloe. This was done with a sledge hammer, which would burr over the top edges of the cog, so enough wood needed to be left there to allow for this. When the cogs were seated then the burred edges were cut off to create a taper from outer edge down to the felloe which allowed the licking cogs to clear each other and so escape. The precision required was so great that the millwrights resorted to filing in the final stages. Each cog involved that much work and the large spur wheel could have 140 of them!

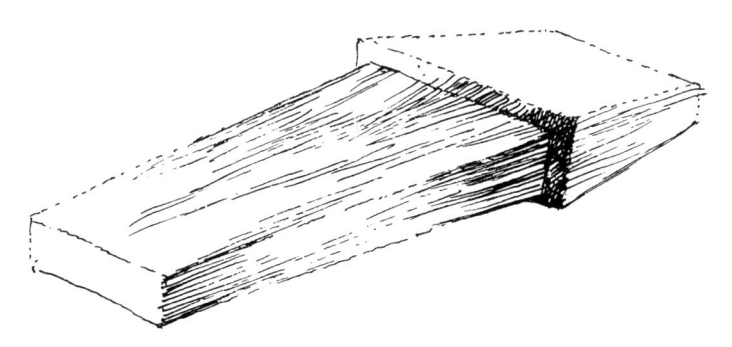

Mill cog

In areas beyond the range of the Hornbeam the millwrights had to use other hard woods, of which fruit wood (Apple and Pear) was preferred. Thus in some lease agreements a miller is required to plant fruit trees at regular intervals. Often this is interpreted in terms of fruit but the prime purpose was to grow, cut and season his own timber, so as to reduce delay in repairing the mill.

Cogs in situ.
Outwood Mill

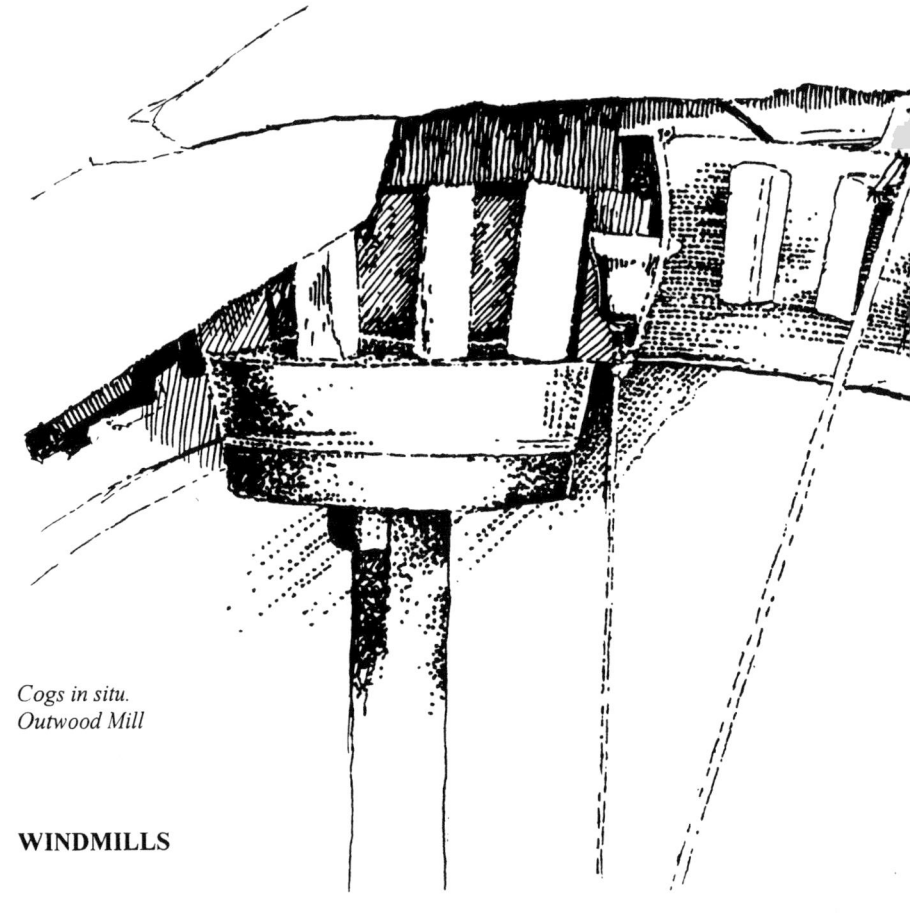

WINDMILLS

To stand on the grass beside the windmill at Outwood in Surrey makes you realise how much bigger it is close-to than it seemed from across the village green. A massive ladder of stairs takes you up to the first machine chamber and you enter the working heart of the mill. Another ladder takes you up again to a confinement of turning cog-wheels. The whole thing is a marvel of engineering. What is not readily appreciated is that the building and its machinery are all balanced upon the top of a great central post that runs vertically up through the whole building. This sounds precarious but in fact the post and the rest are joined so securely that they withstand gales and storms. In the case of Outwood, it has withstood hurricane force winds twice. Nevertheless the construction is so ingenious that the whole building can be rotated around its post - so that the sails can be turned into the wind. Such mills have been around since the 12th century - and we think we're so clever today!

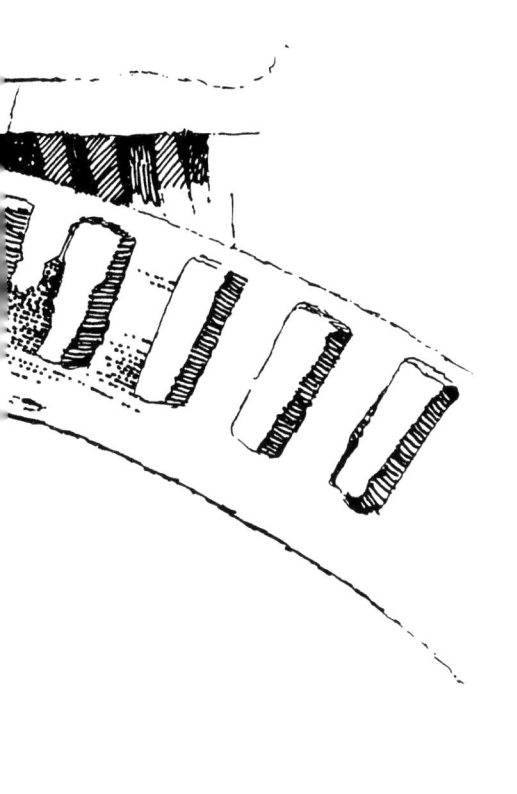

That's not all. When you go and look in the bottom 'roundhouse' of the mill you see the great central post standing in the middle of a massive wooden cross. From the ends of the cross rise lean-to buttresses, called *quarter bars*, which support the post. They do indeed, for they actually hold the post in suspension, to leave a tiny gap between the post and its *cross trees* beneath. Thus the quarterbars take the weight to the outer limits of the structure to ensure its stability. Should you still be in the roundhouse when the mill is turned into the wind there's another surprise in store. It can look as though it's the post that's turning rather than the building - it's an optical illusion![19]

"To climb into the mill when it is working is another experience altogether. But to go into the mill when it was working to a full strong wind was a never to be forgotton experience, for only in that way could its true character be understood and appreciated. To climb the broad oak ladder and go in through the doorway was to enter into the very pulsation of its life. There one was conscious of movement, above, beneath, and around: a quivering of the whole structure, a continuous creaking and rumbling, a sensation of terrific power swaying the whole framework."[20]

---

[19] As an aside, it would seem that this was the principle employed by Hugh Hurley, the master carpenter who built the octagon lantern over the choir of Ely Cathedral. Instead of one central post he framed eight round the space and these supported another sixteen and over this structure he draped the 400 ton lantern, 94 ft above the floor; brilliant!
[20] Rose. Ibid. p.115

Obviously it is crucial for this structuring to have been assembled from the strongest timbers (and there are variations on the design described here). Those that survive today are of Oak and sometimes they are splitting, and are bound in iron. It is said that the earliest ones, in the south east at least, were of Hornbeam which was stronger and wouldn't split. However, it is unlikely that the tree was used much for mills since the trunk normally grows so irregularly it becomes practically impossible to obtain a baulk large and straight enough to use for any sort of constructional work.

It's up in the workings of the mill that Hornbeam came into its own again, and is still employed today if the millwrights can get it. It is used for the cogs just as described for watermills, although the design principles have to be inverted since the driving force enters at the top of the mill and has to be transferred down to the millstones beneath. Ratios differ also since the safe working power from wind is not necessarily the same as from water. Most mills needed a wind of at least 10 mph; the maximum varied with the structure of the mill and its gearing. The miller at Outwood has worked it "in half a gale, on the Beaufort scale." About 40 mph was often reported as the maximum for the mill's safety and the miller's nerve. What was vital to the community was that it *did* work. Periods of persistent calm or gale force winds could starve out the people.

It's still a matter of those vital cogs. At Outwood the big brake wheel has 107 cogs and the stone nut 13. Millwrights preferred the number of cogs to be a prime number since that ensured it was not always the same teeth that were in contact with each other and risking uneven wear. They certainly got a lot of wear: a popular ideal was to have the stones rotating 100-120 revs. per min. if they were four foot stones. The smock mill at Shipley, West Sussex, is so geared that one revolution of the sails causes eleven revolutions of the stones and as it works well with the sails revolving fifteen times a minute so the stones turn at 165 revs. per min. That means the tips of the sails, being 68 feet apart, are speeding round at 60 mph.

The prime ideal was to balance speed (and therefore flour production) with safety. If the miller doesn't understand the running of the machinery the stones can cause sparks and set everything alight. Fire in

Outwood Mill, Surrey.
Built 1665; local tradition has it that the workman could see, in the northern sky, the glow from the Great Fire of London!

mills was a constant fear and one which, from time to time, was fulfilled. Safety also depended upon the skill of the craftsmen who built and maintained the mill. One of the greatest hazards was the breaking of a cog. George Medhurst of Lewes in Sussex was one of the noted Victorian millwrights and recently at Shipley, when some cogs needed renewing it was found that the old ones, of Beech, were all signed by him and dated 1872 - they'd certainly been made to last!

THE MUSICIAN
GENERAL

Many an old country house has at least one beautiful musical instrument on display, silent and roped off from the public.[21] Quite probably the guide informs that it was brought back from the Grand Tour or some similar great adventure. Indeed, in terms of the development of early music and instruments we need to look very much towards the Continent. It's hardly surprising, then, that Hornbeam appears on lists of timbers for musical instruments. We thought immediately of the woodwind section but as it turned out, it has been more important for keyboard instruments.

Any wood chosen must retain its shaping so remarkably as to keep the instrument in tune. Furthermore, it must not be too sensitive to changes in the room atmosphere: woodwind instruments can go sharp while keyboard instruments can go flat. The hardness of Hornbeam suggests it would be an ideal candidate. However, The Horniman Museum reported back that they have no such instruments in their collections but they had spoken to a present-day craftsman-musician who had worked with Hornbeam. He had used it as a substitute for Box as part of the make-up of some wind instruments - an idea given him by a German craftsman. Fortunately there are craftsmen today who can recreate the old instruments, although not necessarily using the original choice of woods. Some have even been available in kit form, such as harpsichords from John Storrs Workshops, where they employed Hornbeam for the jacks and bridges. Like other craftsmen, they reported that the timber is scarce and difficult to find, but *"Luckily, you don't need much for a jack tongue. We've used about half of the tree we bought ten years ago."*

KEYBOARD INSTRUMENTS

Several sources list Hornbeam for 'hammer heads for early pianos and harpsichords.' This is misleading. Harpsichords do not have hammer heads. What the instruments have in common is a need for white keys

---

[21] two exceptions where you can sometimes hear them played: Finchcocks Living Museum of Music, Goudhurst, Kent and the Cobbe Collection housed by the National Trust at Hatchlands, Surrey.

*Sketches of craftsmen
Working on harpsichords,
Dolmetsch workshops, 1980*

and the pale timber of the Hornbeam has supplied that demand. What is noticeable is that organs never appear on the lists despite having white keys and being coeval with the other two. A strong timber, such as Hornbeam, would have been needed for early organ keyboards since they were played with the fists!

The ideal was to cut as many keys as possible from the same piece of timber, and to keep them in the same order, so that the grain matched. You might imagine that changing from one plank to the next would be made to happen *between* the keys but some craftsmen organised the join down the centre of a key. They crafted that join so perfectly that you've got to search for it. High standards indeed, but these were applied to all materials. The white keys were more universally made from expensive Box wood, ivory and bone, than from Hornbeam. It may have fallen from favour for expensive instruments because the wood darkens with age – judging by the items shown to us at Kew.

The black keys were of stained hardwood, usually one of the fruitwoods (Apple, Pear, etc.), until the opening up of the New World and the importation of Ebony. These choices remained popular with French and German craftsmen up to the 1790s. Flemish craftsmen were choosing Oak with bone by 1580.

To have white keys for the 'naturals' and black keys for the 'sharps' only became the norm about 1800; on early instruments the arrangement could be the reverse. The present day arrangement of five raised and seven natural keys was standardised far earlier - right back in the 15th century[22]. The size and number of the keys has changed too. Early organs had very wide keys but stringed instruments were narrower. They were very similar to today's, with the naturals less than an inch wide giving an octave span of seven inches. On a modern piano it's six inches. So it was on Italian and Flemish harpsichords from the 16th to 18th centuries. English ones, at that time, were three eighths of an inch wider. By the 18th century most French and German instruments had the narrower span of six and a quarter inches - and this permitted the playing of tenths. The size of keys was thus crucial, dictating the number of octaves and what could be played.

There was only a single octave available on some early instruments, such as organs, but this had increased to two and a half, or three, in the 15th century. This went up to four or four and a half in the 16th century and by the 18th century it was common to have five (except in Italy and Spain). By 1818 Beethoven was composing for six and a half[23]. There were seven before 1830 and now a modern piano of 88 keys provides seven and a third.

PIANOS

The crucial date in the evolution of the piano is 1709 - the year when Bartolomeo Cristofori, in Florence, perfected the basic mechanism of all subsequent pianos. It says in some texts that Hornbeam became favoured for the hammers because it was heavy - the key fell back into place promptly, ready for replaying. This is disputed. The mechanism worked faster than waiting for gravity to return the key. The importance of the weight lies in the density of the wood which affects the sound. It is also said that the hammers were made of this wood for its hard wearing qualities but the hammers were covered with leather (felt today) and so were not taking the wear directly. What lies behind the statement is the hard-wearing point that Hornbeam provides; it won't crumble. That's not always the case with the popular alternative

---

[22] with the two exceptions of the short octave and the divided sharps.
[23] Requirement of his Hammerclavier Sonata Opus 106 completed in that year.

choice of imported Sapele.[24] Various woods have been tried, especially the fruitwoods, but from the 19th century the preferred choice became Hornbeam[25].

That has persisted. Thus a 1956 survey[26] reported, "For the small parts of the action (jacks, levers, butts, butt-shanks, etc.) all the firms were using Hornbeam. Maple had been preferred in the past, but at the time when supplies were difficult the change to hornbeam, which was often used on the Continent, was made. The design of some of the small parts is very complicated and it is not practicable to plane them, so it is necessary to use a timber which gives a good finish off a very fine saw. The wood also has to bore well, taking small holes cleanly and at close centres and must remain stable, as swelling would cause jamming of the

---

[24] *Entandrophragma cylindricum*; better known as one of the choices for panelling in the old British Rail trains.
[25] Pers. Com. Curator, Finchcocks – Living Museum of Music; Goudhurst, Kent.
[26] Pearson, F.G.O. and Webster, Constance; *Timbers used in the Musical instruments Industry*; Forest Products Research Laboratory, for Ministry of Technology, 1956, repr. 1967.

action. *Hardness and the ability to hold screws are also essential factors. These requirements are exacting and the makers were fairly satisfied with hornbeam, provided that it was carefully selected. The main difficulty encountered was the tendency to cupping of the boards and this frequently caused trouble in the early stages of manufacture. Two firms used French hornbeam and a third home-grown material when it was available, supplementing it with French.*

The report continues with a closer review of the hammers, reporting that although manufacturers had gone over to Canadian Rock Maple (*Acer saccharum,*, better known as the Sugar Maple) there was still one using hammers with shanks made from Hornbeam, imported from Germany. For the heads, there were five popular choices, including Hornbeam, but regarding this, the writers encountered contradictory views: "*Hornbeam was considered by many to be too heavy, though others preferred it.* This is still a matter of debate today with pages of correspondence on the Internet, at the time of writing.

HARPSICHORDS

With harpsichords, the Hornbeam feature is the wooden *jack* which is operated by the key. It bears the plectrum that plucks the string. This makes a quiet sound and so after about 1590 each key was given two jacks to pluck at least two strings and thereby increase the volume. More Hornbeam for keys and jacks was needed for the next development which was to double the keyboard with a second *manual*. This is thought to have been played independently of the first but there is some doubt. This design was available in Flanders before 1620. It increased the musical possibilities but there were still frustrating limitations so in the 1640s the French redesigned it. Two-manual versions became widespread throughout Europe during this century. In the following century the Germans added more strings and picks per key. Indeed, designers have tried variations on all these ideas through the three or four centuries but always the harpsichord has retained its own distinctive sound, simply because it is plucked. It's always quieter than a piano and so fell from favour but only until the end of the 19th century. During that great age of enquiring into everything, there were people whose imaginations were caught by early instruments and their music. Out of these enquiries arose the modern revival.

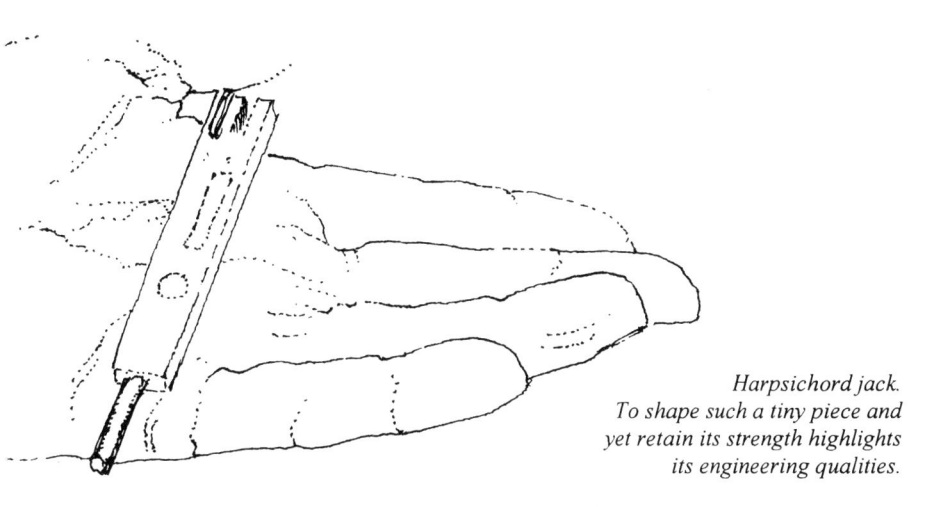

*Harpsichord jack.
To shape such a tiny piece and
yet retain its strength highlights
its engineering qualities.*

Arnold Dolmetsch (1858-1940) rises above the others, not only for his personal world-wide influence, but because his family continue the work today. So do others whom he inspired and craftsmen who were trained in the Dolmetsch workshops: *'He deserves to be considered the 'godfather' not only of the present British school of harpsichord-making, but also of the flourishing American school...'*[27]

Born at Le Mans in France, he worked in Paris, Boston (USA) and London from where he settled at Haslemere in Surrey in 1918. His interest and enthusiasm had been captured by a wide range of early instruments and their special sounds that he not only learned to appreciate but to play to a high performance level. Of course, without the modern benefit of electronic recording, he had to learn for himself how the ancient instruments could be played and how their musicality could be expressed. His personal style became highly influential, through his public performances, not least of which were at Haslemere where he founded the *Haslemere Music Festival* in 1925. It is still an annual event, making it the music festival in Britain that has run longest without a break.

Upon the death of Arnold in 1940, his son Carl took over the directorship until his own death at 85 in 1997. He had played in the very first festival and played in 71 more. In 1999 he was commemorated by the planting of a Tulip Tree in the grounds of Haslemere Museum, during the celebrations of the 75th festival.

---

[27] Encyc. Britannica; 15th ed.; 1997.

Elsewhere in the town Dolmetsch workshops were established to recreate the instruments - many a reader must have played a Dolmetsch recorder at primary school. Here too, in their designs from the workshop, there was Dolmetsch style and influence. Since his death the family has continued the work through a wide range of instruments, from lutes and viols to clavichords.

PIPES AND DRUMS

Home-grown Hornbeam has been tried for drumsticks but rejected because the grain isn't always straight enough and it tends to become brittle. Hornbeam from France is more suitable but there are problems over supply. Similarly, it has been tried for bagpipes, along with Apple and Holly, but rejected, for although they are suitably fine textured to take a good finish they nevertheless tend to split. Until foreign timbers, such as African Blackwood, were imported there was no alternative to using these British woods.[28]

******

THE PLOUGHMAN

We can still feel something very satisfying when the plough cuts the stubble and turns the rich dark soil. It's always been that way. Ancient writers like Pliny and Vetruvius must have watched the same. It was they who recorded that oxen were harnessed to the plough with a yoke made of Hornbeam. That usage came to Britain and was long lasting – up to the 1940s.

The yoke was a massive, heavy, beam, shaped to fit across the shoulders of a pair of oxen. It therefore needed to be some twelve feet long. Each yoked pair was known as a *yoke of oxen* and so records of there being four yokes to a team mean there were eight animals. Such a team was standard although they did vary from one to six yokes. The alternative was to work a mixture of oxen and horses together in the same team. This has been done since horses were first used for ploughing, back in the early Middle Ages and continued well into the age of photography. However, trying to work one of each, as a pair, poses difficulties for harnessing owing to their different anatomical

---

[28] Pearson and Webster; pp 35 and 32 resp.

designs; collars are used on horses and yokes on oxen. All the same, in places like the Cotswolds and Wiltshire oxen did work in collars. Horses could well choke in an ox yoke as it would compress the jugular vein and the windpipe. This is shown happening, it's believed, in the famous horse carvings on the Parthenon where they are throwing back their heads, to prevent strangulation. Greeks and Romans, it was thought, must have adopted an ox yoke in their early workings with draught horses – a point seemingly confirmed, in 1910, when tested by the French cavalry officer, Lefevre des Noettes.

The yoke was secured to the oxen using wooden bows that looped round their throats. These bows were usually made of Ash as it is not only strong but pliant enough to meet the challenge and retain a degree of 'give' to allow for effective working. Indeed, a comment from

Evelyn implies that he believed even the intractable Hornbeam of the yoke had 'give' in it: *"it was as well flexible as tough."*[29]

Chains from a central hook under the yoke secured the oxen to the plough and for other draught purposes a central pole or even shafts were used. With those attachments made, work could begin. A team could plough about 40 rods, poles or perches without a pause. That's the original 'furrow long' that became a 'furlong,' now standardised to 220 yards or one eighth of a statute mile. When the parallel furrows covered a square furlong then some ten statute acres had been ploughed. There's about eleven miles of furrow to the acre (depending upon the closeness of the furrows of course) and that was a day's work for an eight ox team.

Each team worked best with two 'ploughmen': one who drove the plough and another at the head of the team. The most experienced oxen worked at the front, and if there was only one he was placed on the off side. The next grade worked immediately in front of the plough and trainees were worked in the middle.[30]

Individually, oxen were slower than horses by some 50%, even though both can exert about the same pull. A horse can achieve 432 foot pounds per second whereas an ox can only manage 288, (there are 500 to a standardised horsepower). Don't forget oxen were more determined, especially on heavy soils that defeated horses. Some areas, in Devon and Sussex for example, remained devoted to the ox. The debate between the two would probably have been settled centuries ago, in favour of the horse, if it had not been for the highly influential writings of Walter of Henley in the 13th century. He was an ox champion and set out costings to prove his point. They were accurate, judging from other sources, until it came to shoeing. There he exaggerated grossly the cost of shoeing horses. In short, both animals have qualities for ploughing. Speed or tenacity aside, it was the weather and the land that would determine what animal was best for any given day. The seasons would move on relentlessly and there was little time to wait for the soils to dry out. The ploughing *had* to be done. The whole community depended upon the next crop.

---

[29] Evelyn. *Silva.* p.48
[30] see Fussell, Trow-Smith, Urquhart and Whitlock in bibliography

SPORTS AND GAMES

BALLS

There is a wide range of games and sports requiring a hard ball and some of these have come to light in the search for Hornbeam, which is no surprise bearing in mind the wood's weight, resistance to impact and reluctance to split. In the case of bowls there is no doubt what the recorders had in mind but with golf and billiards it could be the clubs and cues that were intended, and most probably this was the case. With skittles both balls and pins were meant. No information specific to the other games has been found so far but once Hornbeam was recognised as a good timber from which to make balls it is likely to have been used whenever a really hard ball was needed.

"LET'S TO BILLIARDS"

So said Shakespeare's 'Cleopatra' to her handmaiden, Charmian. When Charmian declines Cleopatra retorts *"As well a woman with an eunuch play'd / as with a woman."* which suggests this was always a male orientated game. At least Shakespeare expected a good audience response from the quip![31] It dates from 1591 and is the earliest English reference, according to the Oxford English Dictionary. There are earlier European references to the game, from the 15th century, but where the game started is not known for certain; claims are made by France, England, China, Italy and Spain!

When earlier writers listed 'billiards' as a use for Hornbeam they probably meant the cues as there is a link between them and the name 'billiards'. A 'roundwood' length cut from pollards and coppice stools (including Hornbeam) as fuel was called a *billet* and firewood is still called billets today, even if more like quartered logs than roundwood. *Billet* came from the Latin *billa* or *billus* which meant a branch or trunk and that in turn was of Celtic origin - hence *bille* in Irish for a sacred large tree. It would seem that some of those straight, roundwood lengths were made into the cues. The notion that the cue got its name from a William Kew is not supported by the OED.

---

[31] Anthony and Cleopatra Act 11, Sc.5,1.3.

Modern cues are composite with the butts likely to be made from Rosewood (*Dalbergia spp.*) or Ebony (*Diospyros spp.*) while the shafts are likely to be of Ash (*Fraxinus excelsior*), Maple *(Acer spp.)* or Ramin (*Gonystylus bancanus*). As for the balls - the first plastic one was made in 1868 - the first anything to be made of plastic.[32]

BOWLS, SKITTLES and TEN PIN BOWLING

About 5,200 years ago an Egyptian family placed a set of skittles in the tomb of their child and those provide the oldest evidence for the game. They were of stone, not wood, and it looks as though the child had to bowl through an archway of marble at the skittle pins. No doubt there were many such games in the days when hunting or driving predators from livestock were all important, since they are basically 'target practice'. In due course they became ritualised, so that evidence from early Germany has Christians 'killing' pagans - the Germans carried wooden clubs called *kegels*[33] for self-protection but they had to leave them in the cloister when they went to church. They stood them up against the wall to represent pagans and rolled stone balls at them. A strike meant the bowler was cleansed of sin.

Thus this was one game that the Church endorsed; Martin Luther built a skittle alley for his children and played himself. It was held in high esteem too; the banquets of the upper classes had entertainments between the numerous courses and the record of a 1463 German

---

[32] Lewington, Anna; *Plants for People*; The Natural History Museum; 1990; p.216.
[33] a word still used sometimes in the game.

banquet has the guests playing bowls after the venison course. It became serious too - in 1325 both Berlin and Cologne restricted the betting to five shillings while a 1518 competition at Breslau[34] awarded a whole ox to the winner. Gambling was to have a major influence on the game for centuries to come.

From Germany in the 15th century the game spread to Austria and Switzerland and then the Low Countries so that it was soon across the North Sea to Britain. No doubt Dutch and Flemish traders played it in the ports while they were waiting for the tide to turn. Permanent 'lanes' were established, either with planks to bowl along or of smooth clay, coated with ashes when wet, and it was wet so often in London that the practice of roofing the lanes originated there. That was in c.1455 for lawn bowls; the development of the game branched in two directions, which we would now distinguish as bowls and skittles, but it's not always clear in the old records which version was being bowled. The English liked bowls and took that version to America while the Dutch preferred bowling at pins and took that game to America, both in the 17th century.[35] The English preferred palm-held bowls while the Dutch introduced the thumb holes.

The number of pins wasn't important. They have ranged from three to seventeen but when the diamond formation rose in popularity so nine became standard and the game became known as 'nine pin bowling'. The levels of gambling in America far outstripped Europe and became such a major concern in America, especially on the Sabbath, that anti-gambling laws were introduced to control nine pin bowling. It is said that the tenth pin was added so as to evade these laws but that does not stand up to scrutiny. When the State Legislature of Connecticut banned the game in 1841 they called it Nine Pins but added, "whether more or less than nine-pins are used." It was called Ten Pins in a ban from a month earlier, at Perry in New York State. There had always been versions of the game with ten pins, as shown in a painting of 1810 depicting a game at Ipswich, England, where there had been Flemish immigrants for well over a century and traders for hundreds of years before that, bringing in versions from the Continent.

---

[34] now Wroclaw in Poland.
[35] Timbers other than Hornbeam used in America; Yew (*Taxus* spp.) was one popular choice.

In England nine pins became standard for skittles just as the pins and balls came to have regional standards. The pins weighed about 8lb each while the balls weighed 10lb. That was in the Midlands and the West Country. In London they didn't use balls but round flattened 'cheeses' weighing 12-14lb. These were hurled at the skittles from twenty feet away and yes, there was a net at the end.[36]

Bowls - without the pins - changed from using Hornbeam once new timbers became available from the Americas. One in particular has dominated the scene and that was the 'wood of life' or, in Latin, Lignum vitae (*Guaiacum officinalei*) from the West Indies, Colombia and Venezuela. It is so dense that it's 70-80% heavier than Oak, making it the world's heaviest timber in commercial use and more than capable of withstanding a game of bowls. Indeed it's so dense it resists abrasion too and remains the perfect bowl needed for those tense winning moments. It has a very high resin content which makes the wood waterproof, so the weight stays the same and the shape doesn't distort.[37] Hornbeam and other hard woods used in the early days of bowls played roles of vital social importance. Bowls became such a high status game that bowling greens had to be licensed from the king. That's why we're told Sir Francis Drake was playing bowls before the Armada - not to show he was so calm but to show that his host was held in such high esteem that the king granted such a licence.

GOLF

There's a little chap in yellow hose and a smart white linen tunic with gold neckband taking a swipe at a misshapen 'ball' with what looks like a hockey stick, in the great medieval east window of Gloucester Cathedral.[38] He's often described as a golfer but there were a number of medieval stick-and-ball games, which he could equally well be playing. If he is a golfer then he is the earliest on record for the glazing of the window was probably completed in 1357. The OED gives the earliest written reference to the word golf as 1457.

---

[36] Entry developed mainly from entries in *Encyclopaedia Britannica* and the *Children's Britannica*.
[37] Lewington. pp.217-8
[38] see Cathedral guide books or captioned colour photo in *Stained Glass* by Lee Lawrence., Seddon, George, and Stephens, Francis; Mitchell Beazley; 1976.

Establishing the use of Hornbeam for golf clubs proved one of the great challenges of this book. Manufacturers, in Britain and the USA, denied this usage so often we began to believe them. Then Kew informed us that in their collections they had one! They have too! It's a smart little putter head with a 8cm striking surface, labelled as coming from the Army and Navy Co-operative Society. Thus we were able to return to museums and manufacturers and push harder for them to check their records and book shelves. Thus we are able to offer the following outline.

Early players of such games used whatever was to hand but as distinct games developed (and with them wagers!) so materials were selected more discerningly. A wide range of timber has been selected for golf clubs, usually such fruitwoods as Apple, Pear, Plum and Cherry but also Beech, Dogwood,[39] Blackthorn or Hawthorn, Holly and Yew. It was the Blackthorn that was grown specially, *"for while it is hard enough to wear well, there is not that stony hardness, which is sometimes found in holly, hornbeam, rockwood, etc."*

It was not just the qualities of the wood in relation to hitting the ball that had to be taken into account but the weather also. Excessive wet could ruin clubs as could striking frozen ground, hence the development of golf in eastern rather than western Scotland, where the climate was drier and links near sea level were less prone to heavy frost:

"When one considers that it could be ruination to one's clubs to play on a wet day (and it must be remembered that in the days of the feather ball, the ball became a sodden mass of feathers as well), that it was not advisable to play on a frosty day, that striking the ball in the heel of the club might well fracture the neck in the days of the gutty ball, and that, moreover, the club required constant attention, drying, oiling, etc. and when one then considers the number of wet and frosty days in Scotland in any one year, it is clear that the golf-playing Scot had an enthusiasm bordering on the fanatical for his chosen game."[40]

It's not surprising that Hornbeam gets listed for golf clubs since its density makes it superbly resistant to impact, for the head, and its

---

[39] Not the British shrub but its American relative, *Cornus florida*.
[40] Henderson, Ian T. and Stirk, David I.; *Golf in the Making*; Arnold; 1982; P.141.

strength, for the handle. A more shock absorbent timber might have been more comfortable for the handle and indeed when composite clubs evolved Ash was chosen. However, British timbers have their shortcomings; it was reported in 1905 that, *"Hornbeam has merits of its own, but it is rather given to develop serious cracks or shakes in seasoning, and yew has the same peculiarity"*[41]. Thus the 19th century saw these British woods disappearing in favour of two American alternatives. Firstly Hickory (*Carya spp.*) from America became popular after the 1840s and 1850s. Legend has the first Hickory arriving in Dundee harbour as ballast in a ship from Russia. By 1890 it was the prime timber, supplanting Ash. Then in 1896 America started sending their Persimmon (*Diospyros virginiana*)[42] club heads at the rate of 100,000 a year. It's still in use today. Therefore the foreign timbers were found to have qualities that surpassed that of the British native trees.[43]

Balls have been made from Hornbeam but no reference has been traced to date that's specific to *golf* balls. Golfers might like to know that the white latex on the best balls today also comes from a tree - the Balata (*Manilkara bidentata*) from Tropical America.

BOARD GAMES

Chess and draughts have both had their pieces made from Hornbeam, just as it has been used for dominoes and Scrabble counters.

---

[41] quoted in Ellis, Jeff.; *The Clubmakers's Art*; Zephyr; 1997; p316.
[42] Henderson p. 143
[43] Inf. also from British Golf museum and Lewington, Anna; *Plants for People*; The Natural History Museum; 1990; pp. 216-8

THE THRESHER

THRESHING FLOORS AND FLAILS

In Hornbeam country the great barns were regularly constructed with two short cross arms like the transepts of a cruciform church. These held the main doors which were thus opposite each other and by opening both sets a good through-draught could be achieved. This was necessary for processing the corn. The stooks were brought into the central space between the doors, either from stacks down the main body of the barn or from the rickyard outside, and there they would be threshed - have the grains of corn separated from straw and chaff. The straw was forked to one side and the grain tossed into the air for the through-draught to blow aside the light chaff. The heavier grain fell straight back down. Nowadays all that's done by the combine harvester out in the field.

The work area for threshing had to be clean, so the earth floor itself was not suitable. Sometimes it was paved but that was not ideal since beating the corn on stone could crush the grains. Better, was a wooden floor of great planks. It provided an even surface but had to be of a hard timber that would resist the beating, so as not to leave indents where grains could shelter. Oak was a regular choice but, where available, Hornbeam was often preferred. Otherwise Sycamore might be used for the sake of the even compactness of its grain, or Wych Elm for its tough resistance to splitting or Ash for its tensile strength and natural springiness. Whatever the choices, the favoured timber would be the one least likely to release raised sections or splinters of wood damaged by the flail, since these would impede the shovels scooping up the corn. So important was the need to keep this surface as smooth and perfect as possible that not only was it given a protective covering when not in use but workers had to change their clogs or boots for soft footwear to safeguard both the wood and the grain. It was practically sacred, as recalled by Walter Rose:[44] *"The threshing floor was jealously guarded from profane use; the men who cleaned and sacked the threshed corn wore felt slippers in order to avoid crushing the grain."*

---

[44] Rose, Walter; *The Village Carpenter*; CUP; 1937; p 69.

When carpenters made a new floor they expended enormous effort to get the timbers fitting side by side as perfectly as possible. Ill-fitting joins would admit grains of corn to be crushed and waste flour. Then a build up of this waste would force the joins apart and increase the problem. To reduce this risk they preferred planks taken from the same tree so that any natural curvature would be repeated in the neighbouring timber, enabling them to snuggle together as closely as possible. Hornbeams can have a lot of this natural curvature. The keen eye of the craftsmen spotted this potential in the raw material before striving with saw and axe to make it virtuous. What striving it must have been against the unyielding, unforgiving toughness of the Hornbeam. When it looked good the sides were fitted with angle-irons into joists to prevent sideways spreading of the timbers and the opening up of cracks. Lastly, wedges were driven in between the irons and the timbers and adjusted round the floor to ensure the tightest of perfect fits.

The flail that was used against the corn on the threshing floor was, in simple terms, two straight sticks coupled loosely together. Descriptions from the end of their period of usage say each piece was about an *ell* long but earlier illustrations often show the head shorter than the handle. An ell was a variable measurement that became standardised in England to 45 inches (37.2 inches in Scotland). In practice it was the length from the holding hand to the tip of the nose when the face was turned away from the holding hand. Ash was used for the handle with Blackthorn, Hawthorn or Hornbeam for the head.

The tool was swung through the air to give impetus to the head as it was brought down upon the corn. The intention was only to dislodge the grain from the ears and straw, not to split the grains open or crush them into the floor. The thresher learnt through experience how much energy he need expend and how much to save, for the relentless swinging and bending of arms and body made this an exhausting task. This was something the normally astute Gertrude Jekyll forgot completely when she recorded with nostalgic romanticism: *"The threshing of corn on the barn floor was one of the happiest of country sights and sounds. From after harvest to the spring of the next year, stored in the ample bays of the barn, it could be threshed out as it was wanted, hand-winnowed, and put away in the granary."*[45] Yet she obviously knew there was an art to it, for while recording at the same time the flailing of oats she says: *"It was threshed out, a little at a time, by one of the few labourers who could still use the tool..."*[46].

Although a threshing machine was invented by Andrew Meikle c.1784 the flail continued in use into the 20th century and was brought back into use when there was no fuel for machines during the Second World War. Towards the end of the 19th century a flail cost only 6d but the labour charge incurred for its use meant that a new steam thresher could do the job for less than half the cost.[47]

******

THE TURNER

What wonderful warm woody smells linger in memories of the turner's workshop. So often it's just a woody smell to most of us but the experienced woodworker can tell one tree from another just by the scent. Pine, of course, has that distinctive resinous smell, just as a mushroomy smell tells of Birch that was infected with Birch Bracket Fungus. There's often a fruity smell from Cherry, sometimes reminiscent of pineapple, sometimes of almonds, even said to be of laudanum! It takes a hard sniff with Hornbeam, since it doesn't have much scent at all - until the finishing stages. Then as the wood heats under the pressure of sanding it does produce a distinctive smell. That's a warning. If Hornbeam is treated too firmly at this stage it will 'check' or produce a crazed surface of little cracks.

All manner of small objects can be worked by the turner out of Hornbeam – usually egg cups and serviette rings today. Most village

---

[45] Jekyll, Gertrude; *Old West Surrey*; Longmans; 1904; p. 187.
[46] Jekyll. p 23.
[47] Fussell, G.E.; *The Farmers' Tools*; Bloomsbury Bks ed. 1985; p. 174.

turners have, traditionally, always had a wide range of skills – it's all very well turning chess pieces but little horse heads have still got to be made for the knights! It's just such the case with the subject of this chapter, which concentrates on one larger item - the screw. Think not of the little metal fastenings of today but big wooden screws – one, for example, in an 18th century cider press is eleven inches thick. These were the crucial part of wooden presses, for such things as linen, herbs, paper, papyrus, oil seed, and apples for cider. It was the application to the printing press that changed the world.

THE SCREW

Initially, the craftsman had to turn a length of wood into a cylinder. This then had to be marked with the spiral for the screw thread and then that thread was carved by hand. That must have been a slow business, from our viewpoint today, in a world of high-speed power tools. The problem with making these would have been ensuring that the projecting thread was not weakened. There was a danger of revealing too much unsupported 'end grain'. Thus the spiral was kept thick, without too steep an incline and without a sharp edge to the thread.

This is the 'male' part of the device. The craftsman also had to make the 'female' part – the threaded hole into which the other turns and grips. Matching the two sounds highly demanding but present-day craftsmen assured us that this need not have been so. There could have been quite a degree of leeway without the device losing its grip. A tight fit was not crucial.

This was one item we really wanted to see for ourselves but which proved most elusive. Happily, the collections at Kew include a 'bench screw', made entirely of Hornbeam (sketched above). It's 57cm long, of which 36cm are thread. Examples of five other applications and their place in our social history are outlined below.

PRESSES

The first presses were manual without a screw and are thought to date from about 1500 BCE. Each was basically a beam, pivoted at one end so that it acted as a lever, to bring a force down upon a board that pressed whatever was placed underneath it. The force was applied with weights, including the human backside! This advanced to applying force with a screw by the 1st century CE in Europe, although the earlier beam press continued in use. It still did heavy work such as pressing grapes and olives while the screw press took on lesser work, such as pressing herbs and oil seeds. These were used widely for diverse processes, mostly through the same periods of time, rather than one following the other. Of early importance, and perhaps inspirational of all, would have been presses for fruit such as grapes and olives, and in this country, cider apples. However, the cider press is said, sometimes, to have derived from the linen press and that in turn is supposed to have inspired the printing press. It's inclined to go round in circles whereas they are more likely to have been parallel lines of development, taking innovations one from the other to suit different processes. The really revolutionary use in terms of world culture was the invention of the printing press with moveable type.

THE PRINTING PRESS

Early printing began in the Far East, for printing textiles and then for paper. It took nearly a thousand years for it to reach Europe and be taken up with enthusiasm. It required using a separate carved wooden block for each page, which was fine for producing single-sheet Christian images but a daunting challenge for a project as large as the Bible. Then a German goldsmith, with experience of working in the mint, came up with the idea of transferring the notion of the metal dies into moveable type, held in wooden frames, one for each page. He was Johann Gutenberg (1397-1468) working at Strasburg and Mainz. In his day there were only twenty three letters in the alphabet but with capitals, punctuation, abbreviations and multiple symbols he needed about 150 little dies.

He wasn't satisfied with the result. This led him to improve the paper and to dampen it so that it would absorb the ink more evenly and be less prone to slipping. He also improved the ink and the press - changing from the lever version to one with a screw. He's supposed to have got the idea from a linen press. The screw was made for him by a woodturner named Konrad Saspach, according to *The Cologne Chronicle*, written by Ulrich Zell in 1499. He said work on building the new press began in December 1438 and took three weeks to complete.[48] He did not record from which timber the screw was made!

---

[48] see Moran, James; Printing Presses: *A History and Development from the Fifteenth Century to Modern Times*; Faber; 1973.

With it Gutenberg produced one of the world's most famous books, the beautiful Gutenberg Bible (1454).[49] The earliest surviving illustration of one of these presses features in a *Dance Macabre* printed in France, at Lyons in 1499, wherein an animated skeleton is shown grabbing the printer whose head unfortunately obscures the construction of the press, leaving only the top of the screw showing. It remained the prototype of all subsequent screw-type printing presses for four and a half centuries.[50] The screw was changed to metal c.1550 by a Nuremberg craftsman named Danner[51] but otherwise the printing press remained the same until the very end of the 18th century when it became all metal.

The technology was brought to Britain from Cologne by William Caxton. He set up premises at Westminster when he returned to England in 1476 and issued his first book the following year. An example of his design of press, dating from about 1750, belongs to the St. Bride's Printing Library in London - purchased for 50/- in 1894 (viewing by appointment only).

CIDER PRESSES

Screw presses contributed towards the production of cider and that was an all-important drink throughout society, right up to being the chief royal drink, whenever we upset the French and they cut off supplies of red wine.

What we drink today is but a distant cousin of the earlier vintages that disappeared in the 19th century. They're often called 'real cyder' but hereafter we'll just call it cyder. This is the drink that was accepted generally to be the equal of wine at its height, in the 17th century. It was processed in similar ways to wine, in that it matured in casks and bottles. The best vintages were clear in appearance and some, like wine, were best left for several years before consuming. However, farmers and gentlemen who produced cyder across the country soon

---

[49] Illustrated summary in Birdsell, Derek and Cipolla, Carlo M.; *The Technology of Man;* Penshurst Press; 1908.
[50] An important early modification was to stop excessive pressure damaging the type and distorting the print.
[51] Pollock, Michael, *The Performance of the Wooden Printing Press*; Univ. of Chicago Press; 1972.

acquired a taste for the imported wines. Once their attentions were focussed away from cyder the prime vintages disappeared. All that remained were the lesser 'small cider' and 'ciderkin' which were the watered-down drink given to labourers as part of their wages. This is immortalised in those harvest scenes where the workers are taking their hard-earned break. We see them drinking from their little wooden barrels, often called 'harvest bottles' and if these are judged to be about ten inches high then the contents would have been about one gallon. It is from these types of drink that modern commercial cider evolved.

Less well known but more significant than harvest scenes were the rows of cyder barrels on board ships. Water went stagnant but cyder lasted longer. The two could be mixed. Thus important seafaring counties like Devon also became important areas of cyder production. Additionally, cyder kept sailors healthy. They said it helped prevent scurvy and the 1747 recommendation was a pint a day. The validity of this was challenged in our times since cider has none of the vital vitamin C. Defenders of the old cyder were convinced this hadn't been the case in days gone by and eventually proved their point. It's modern processing techniques that destroy the vitamin.

Such skills used to be passed on from generation to generation but with the demise of this system many old cyder-making skills were lost. However, many clues can be gained from the processing of wine, from which techniques were borrowed for cyder in the second half of the 17th century.

In the 17th century the presses were commonly the single screw type and Hornbeam would still have been used. They pressed bundles or 'cheeses' of milled apples. Each bundle was created by folding horsehair sacking over a mass of apple pulp called the *murc*. Otherwise it was called *pummice* from the French *pomace* (from French for apple). It was milled coarsely so that there were few fine particles to clog the mesh. The juices started running before the press was even tightened and this was considered to make the best grade of cyder: *"Which Cyder so obtained, far exceeds that which is forc'd out; as the Wines of France that are unpressed; are by much preferr'd to those that are press'd."*

In Devon they seemed to have perfected this technique. They had some very large cyder presses that could run off a hogshead (54 gallons) of unpressed juice at a time. People were willing to pay a lot extra for this (a crown per hogshead), compared with pressed cyder. The more times the cheese was pressed, and the more times the murc had water added to it, gave the various grades of cyder, just as it did for wine. The weakest became the drink of the working classes and was known as 'small cider' or 'beverage'. Obviously it was also cheapest, which was an important consideration to employers who, by the 18th century, were including this as part of a servant's wages.

LINEN PRESSES

A linen press can be either the cupboard in which linen is stored or else the machine that presses a board down upon laundered linen in order to put an edge to the folds. Why on earth should anybody in the Middle Ages want to invent a machine to make laundering a longer job than it was already? Evidently this concentrated upon table cloths and napkins, and the reason is all to do with status and table etiquette.

So important were the great meals of late medieval and Tudor times that manuals had to be written to ensure all the correct procedures were followed. Sadly, when it comes to the cloths these manuals do not tell the modern reader all that we would want to know. One thing is very obvious. The cloths were highly valued and all guests should respect this. No one should mark the table cloth; wine and gravy stains were not appreciated.

> *Meat nor drink thou not spill*
> *But set it down, both fair and still*
> *Keep thy cloth clean thee beforn*
> *And bear thee so thou have no scorn.*[52]

Thus they were brought out for use on special occasions to impress the guests with their host's wealth at being able to afford such things and also the servants to launder and dress them. These cloths must be thought of in the plural as the tables were often too wide for a single sheet to hang low enough on each side to conceal the trestles; the maximum width of cloth being 63in, dictated by the standard loom. Up to three cloths were needed, laid lengthwise. They were available in grades of quality from coarse to fine. The very finest was reserved for the host at the high table. Guests were seated with the appropriate grade of cloth, according to their social standing, as perceived by the host - you could say a lot with a table cloth! In some households, however, the instructions imply that diners were seated *before* the cloths were laid; such was the case in the household regulations for Henry VII.[53] Again, this may have been to impress people with the number of servants, and man servants at that, since their wages were higher than for women. Serving wenches are the stuff of films.

Two men laid the cloths. They stretched them tight and *straight* between them, which must have been a bit tricky if the guests were already seated. One then used a special rod to smooth out any wrinkles. Contemporary illustrations tend to show the creases on the table top

---

[52] Furnivall, F.J. ed.; *Babees Book, The Boke of Nuture etc.*; Early English Text Society; 1868.
[53] Hammond, P.W. *Food and Fest in Medieval England*; Sutton Publishing; 1993; p.107.

smoothed out, unless the first crease was aligned along the edge, but those in the falls are rendered distinctly.[54]

As for the napkins, these too had to impress and had their own rituals for usage. They were not retained on the lap - they had to be seen! They were draped over the wrist or over the shoulder and of course they had to be smart, which means pressed. Bed sheets had to be pressed too. From medieval and Tudor times the use of the wooden presses continued through Stuart and Georgian times until the end of the 18th century and no doubt some households carried on using them long after that.

OIL SEED PRESSES

I love the fields of brilliant yellow Rape. There's something about them that lifts the spirits but to many people they are a total anathema. Often it is thought of as a new crop, since it's become much commoner from the 1960s but there's nothing new about it. We've been growing Rape for over 600 years.

Pressing seeds to release the oil is one of the world's oldest industries, traceable back 5,000 years to China and Egypt. Most of the famous oil yielding plants such as palms and the olive find it too cold in Britain but several plants can be cropped for their oily seeds. There was Hemp but that was usually grown for fibre. Then there was Flax and that too was grown for fibre (linen) but also for its 'linseed oil'. There were two plants that go down as 'Mustard', White and Black, and two 'Oil Seed Rapes', the fodder version and the turnip-rooted. Early records do not always indicate which oil is being recorded but "on balance" Brace[55] considers that most frequently it is Rape. Whatever the plant, there was a great demand for the oil. It was needed in the processing of the woollen cloth that made England so famous, not to forget its value as a lubricant and a fuel for oil lamps, including street lighting and in soap making. The more savoury edible oils, such as Olive oil, we had to import. In the early Middle Ages we were importing rape seed oil too, or the seed for processing our own. It came from over the North Sea,

---

[54] see illus. Hammond; p. 106 enlarged as the endpapers where distortion in the pattern is shown clearly but the creases are straight and spaced perfectly.
[55] Brace, H.W.; *History of Seed Crushing in Great Britain*; Land Books; 1960.

mainly from Holland, into such ports as Boston and Hull, so that the oil industry centred upon Eastern England.

Thus the earliest reference to making our own oil comes from Lincolnshire where a licence to do so was granted to a certain John Fintour of Crowle by his overlord, who was the Abbot of Selby, in 1381. There is an earlier reference, from Gainsborough in 1377, where Robert Oyler was accused of overcharging but the records do not state whether his oil was imported or home grown.[56]

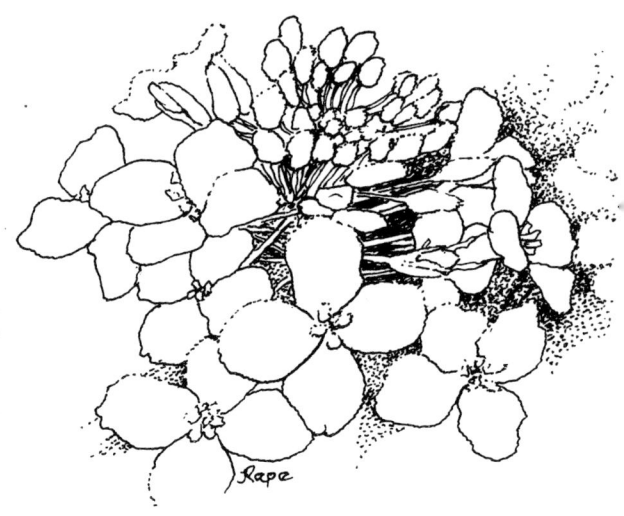

In 1572 a bill was introduced, *"for the making of oils in England. Confirming the Queen's Letters patent granting certain privileges to the inventors of the making of oil out of seeds grown in England equal to the Spanish and foreign oils."*[57]

In other words, there is no truth in the notion that Rape was introduced in the 17th century by Huguenot immigrants[58] or that it was introduced by 17th century Dutch drainage engineers working in the Fens. However, the Huguenots may have been responsible for a re-introduction (perhaps of a better strain) or resurgence of interest in the crop. Rape production has always fluctuated in relation to alternatives. Production probably fell after 1533 when it was enacted that all farmers should grow a quota of flax but that must have been ignored for the next generation revived it in 1563 and the next gave up and repealed it in 1593.[59] Both Flax and Hemp were grown primarily for fibre anyway.

---

[56] ibid p. 15.
[57] ibid - quoted p.15.
[58] there were two main immigrations of French Protestants: after the Massacre of St. Bartholomew in 1572 and in 1685 when Louis XIV repealed the Edict of Nantes that had given them religious tolerance.
[59] Brace p. 16.

None of them is very tasty for culinary uses and cruder uses were eclipsed by whale oil. As whales became scarcer so rape seed oil became increasingly important, especially for oil lamps, until petroleum oil became widespread, after 1859.[60]

Whatever the seeds, they needed 'bruising' to crack their skins in order that the oil could then be pressed out. Originally this would have been done by hand, pounding them in large mortars. For commercial production wind and water mills were employed, crushing *"by breaking it between the two great marble stones of near a tun weight, one standing perpendicularly on the other (they come out of Germany) in mills called oyl-mills.*[61] Then came stamper mills, followed by the hydraulic press. Mechanisation can be traced back to 1571 at least, when Giles Lambarde proposed a device for the clothiers of the woollen industry, to reduce their costs on foreign oils.[62]

Oil working could be a foul job, especially if it was mustard oil, since it releases 'mustard gas'. The men would return home with inflamed, streaming eyes and their flesh blistered and bleeding. They were not safer necessarily if working one of the other crops, such as Rape, since Wild Mustard could be a common weed and become an adulterant in the yield. Even passing a mill could be an unpleasant experience. King James I closed one down: *"Whereas there is an oyle mill erected or used about Tottenham either in the highway or near it, which is so offensive or noysome to his Majestie when he passeth that way as it may not longer be suffered; these are therefore to require you to send for the partie or parties before you that have the use of the mill and straightly to charge or commaund them to leave making those oyles in that place, which presently is to be done, because shortly his Majestie may be occasioned to passe many times that way and if they shall refuse to doe and obey this commaund then wee require and hereby authorise you to see the said mill stayed from working and the parties to be brought before us presently, that we may take such course as shalbe fitt, for which this shalbe your warrant."*[63]

---

[60] Seymour, John; The National Trust Book of Forgotten Household Crafts; Dorling Kindersley; 1987.
[61] 1696. Quoted in Brace p. 10.
[62] ibid p.15.
[63] quoted in Brace p.19.

Pressing for small production could have used the beam or lever presses of ancient origin. The next stage up was to have a wooden screw through the beam, which would exert greater force and was obviously superior to hanging weights on the beam, or sitting the children along it. Alternatively, the beam could be dispensed with and force applied directly from above by screwing down on a pressure board and, for a bigger board, tightening *two* screws down on it. These are the systems that are better known from cider apple presses. They in turn are believed to have been copied from the oil seed presses used by apothecaries extracting oil for their medicines.

WALNUT OIL

It wasn't just small seeds that were pressed for oil but seeds as large as Walnuts. This opens up yet more images of the ways in which our ancestors exploited the simple device of a screw press.

Walnuts (Juglans regia), gathered green in early summer, can yield large quantities of oil: *"For the Oyl, one Bushel of Nuts will yield fifteen Pounds of peeled and clear Kernels, and half as much Oyl, which the sooner it is drawn, is the more Quantity though the drier the Nut the better the Quality; the Lees or Marc of the Pressing [remaining pulp] is excellent for fattening Hogs with,"* reported John Evelyn in the 17th century.[64] He should know; his family estates were at Wotton in Surrey, in which county they claimed to grow the most Walnut trees with the best fruits. The latter point is likely to be good salesmanship! Nevertheless, the Walnut had been grown throughout the Middle Ages[65] and nearly a hundred different uses found for it. Using it as timber was a terrible waste and so that doesn't come into the records until 1585.[66]

The oil is very versatile. Today it is imported for cooking but there's nothing new about that. Evelyn told people to use it for frying or as butter. To make a substitute butter it had to be reduced but it must have been wonderful for people living on hard rye bread or even the rather solid barley-meal bread. The oil would soften the crusts and be much appreciated by those whose teeth had gone. It tasted better too, since

---

[64] *Silva*; p.62. As for the hogs – Evelyn knew about those too since he experimented with selective breeding.
[65] It is not true that the tree was only introduced in the 15th century.
[66] OED.

butter was heavily salted, to preserve it into the winter. Consuming Walnut oil does your insides good and expels tapeworms. No doubt there is a delicate balance here, so take care! The Italians are reputed to have drunk it by the pint to cure pains in their sides but this sounds a bit extreme!

Evelyn records it was used as a polish for walking sticks, and as varnish. It must have been applied thinly as one of its characteristics is the slowness of its drying, especially in colder climates. For this reason it is believed to have been used in the Northern European invention of oil paints for artists, attributed usually to the Van Eycks in the 15th century. It is suitable for delicate colours right down to white and so became important in commercial paint manufacture, still being reported by Brimble in 1948, with special reference to France. In Britain we burnt it as fuel in oil lamps. We used it also in the making of birdlime with which to trap small birds, which lasted until the 1930s. Less certain is the popular belief that gypsies who couldn't provide a son and heir stole a white baby and dyed it brown with walnut oil to convince investigating authorities that it was a gypsy child. This is more likely to be racist propaganda against the Romany people than a regular occurrence.

As the fruits were the prime concern the tree could only be cropped successfully in the southern counties since the catkins are prone to late spring frosts. Thus it would have been far more productive and important during those times when the climate shifted towards being more continental than maritime. Given a frost-free late spring our ancestors could anticipate two harvests: one in early summer to thin the green nuts and a second in autumn for the ripe nuts. It was the thinning harvest that was used for oil. This was timed by traditional lore. People were expected to resist thinning until 12th June and to complete by St. Swithin's Day (15th July). The branches were beaten with long poles and the falling nuts were about an inch in diameter (how fast they must have grown in so short a time since fertilisation). Next they had to be pierced with a needle to test whether the kernel had begun to swell. If the needle passed right through, the fruit was fit for pickling but if the needle hit a kernel then that nut would not pickle successfully and so was quickly sold, eaten or pressed for oil.

THE WHEELWRIGHT

CARTS AND WAGGONS

AXLES

The notion of an old horse drawn cart, clacking and creaking out of a gateway on to a country lane to take its load rattling off to farm or market stirs the emotions. It's like part of a collective memory - in heads too young to remember such things. Unlike so many popular notions of bygone days, this one is basically accurate, right down to the rattle. That told you everything was working well, as outlined below. The following concentrates upon those parts of the vehicles that were made from Hornbeam and the role played by its strengths, rather than being an introduction to the complete structure.[67]

---

[67] For the complete structure, beautifully illustrated, see James Arnold's *Farm Waggons and Carts.*

It doesn't take much imagination to realise that carts and waggons had to be robust. There were no good surfaces. Every route shifted the centre of gravity in all directions as ruts, gullies and potholes, snared with roots and armed with loose stones, had to be negotiated. The wheels were always under terrific stress and so was the axle that bore them. From what has already been said about the strength of Hornbeam it's not surprising that the timber was employed in these structures. It's not the strength of one baulk of timber though. The 'axle' is a construction. It has three parts: the main baulk plus an extending arm added to each end upon which the wheels are hung. Regional names abound for every part of the vehicles but for most of England the main baulk is the *axle bed* (or in Surrey the *exbed*) while the two extensions are either *axle arms* or just *arms*, but called *grease axles* in Gloucestershire. Being a construction means the craftsmanship must be supreme, in order that weakness is not introduced. There must be fidelity in the marriage between form and function.

This was the work of supreme craftsmen - carpenters, wainwrights, cartwrights, wheelwrights, the titles barely matter, as they worked usually in workshop teams, each with particular personal skills but all capable of working with each other. For century after century they have made and repaired sound vehicles with no personal need for literacy or numeracy - "*Measurement he had none; but his eyes knew*".[68]

Hornbeam provided the strength for the axle bed, which, although as many feet long as the width of the body, might only be five and a half inches square. Prime Beech will do this too and became the usual choice once the tree had become widespread. In the early days it was a greater rarity than Hornbeam and so it is presumed Oak was used. Whatever the choice, it must be a timber that would retain its rigidity over the years; a good axle bed of wood will only bend slightly, unlike the iron that eventually replaced it. Another consideration, which both Hornbeam and Beech fulfil admirably, is resistance to impact. Should the wheels straddle a tree stump that's been cut too high to allow clearance then the sudden jolt can injure seriously both horse and workman and wreck the vehicle. That's one reason why cartwheels can be so big. Their hubs (alias naves or stocks) raise the axle bed to the

---

[68] Sturt, George; The Wheelwright's Shop; 1923 (1963 ed. used; p. 135).

same height as themselves but of course that's still only half the diameter of the wheel. In some designs the front wheels are smaller than the rear and these obviously dictate clearance - particularly important when driving over the stools of a freshly cut coppice.

The wheels were not fitted directly on to the ends of the axle bed but on to those extensions called axle arms. This is where a particularly clever bit comes in, for although we might presume that these extended in line with the axle bed, this was not in fact the case. They deviated from the square, being made to point downwards slightly and forwards slightly. These deviations were essential for the long life of the wheels.

To understand this, firstly, visualise a wheel and notice it is *dished* - in other words the spokes project at an angle, a little outwards from the hub to the rim. Now visualise the wheel turning slowly, so there's chance to notice the path taken by a chosen spoke. Notice that as it revolves down so it passes through the point where it is exactly perpendicular between the hub and the ground. There's the wonder. It *is* vertical - so what's happening to the angle of the dish? Look at the top of the wheel and see how it is being thrown out from the side of the cart to tilt that bottom spoke down into a vertical position. Here the force is end-on and so it will bear much more weight than if it is still dished at an angle. This tilt is created by the axle arms deviating from the square.

Thus a revolving wheel is constantly shifting position. This is called *foreway*. It keeps carts going safely for years. To enable it to happen the wheels must be able to move up and down their axle arms. To aid this the arms are made to taper, from five inches to three inches, but the wheels do not come off the end because a linch pin blocks their progress. When the wheels spin back along the arms they are blocked by shoulders on the inside to prevent the wheels crashing against the cart side. Thus the wheel doesn't simply go round and round but also moves along its axle arm (called running *off and back*). It clicks against the linch pin and knocks against the shoulder to make that noise peculiar to such vehicles but which also proclaims that all is working as it should. Plenty of lubrication is needed.

There are two more good reasons why this scheme evolved. Firstly, it's a way of absorbing safely the uneven stresses put on the wheels crossing rough ground, and, secondly, it accommodates the lateral swagger of a walking horse which is transmitted down the shafts and through to the wheels. All this is achieved by fitting the arms a fraction of an inch out of square - about three sixteenths of an inch to be precise - to make the wheels slightly 'pigeon-toed'. Fine judgement indeed but when it's a four wheeled waggon there's the added challenge, which must be met, to ensure that the rear wheels follow in exactly the same track as the front ones. Not only was this utterly precise for any given waggon but according to Sturt[69] was apparently exactly the same for all waggons in a given region no matter which workshop made them.

Then in 1803 case-hardened iron was introduced and adopted for making the arms. The axle beds could now be made slightly slimmer but there was argument that wheels didn't run so well on iron as they did on wood - a point still asserted during the research for this section. By this time though the arms were most often sheathed in iron anyway so that the wheels were already turning iron on iron.

HUBS

Today, the centre of a wheel is invariably called the *hub* but in earlier times there were regional variations. *Hub* was used in the South Midlands in counties such as Oxford and Northampton, while *nave* was used in the East Midlands (Lincolnshire) and in Hertfordshire, Sussex and Kent, while *stock* was used in Surrey and the West Midlands (Cotswolds and Gloucestershire)[70]

When it came to making one, the choice of timber was crucial. The block of wood had to be so resistant to splitting that the mortices for the tenons of the spokes could be cut into it, all the way around, without it splitting. More importantly, it had to withstand the forces from the spokes bearing the load, without splitting. The prime material was English Elm as it has a wavy grain that makes it particularly resistant. Even better was the bur sawn off the trunk of a mature Elm. The grain

---

[69] Ibid. p. 136.
[70] Arnold. p. 11.

in one of those was twisted all round, making it impossible to split. Alternatives were Hornbeam and Oak, and these, for complete reassurance against splitting, were bound with an iron bond by the wheelwright.

******

THE WOODSMAN

When the traditional woodsmen stepped back to allow a great tree to crash to the woodland floor ahead of them they did so having used only axes and wedges – no saws. These skills persisted, on a commercial level, well into the 20th century and are among our oldest since they began with flint axes in the Stone Age. Man soon learned to axe out a notch low to the ground facing the direction of fall. Then round the 'back' of this they axed away at an ever increasing notch at a slightly higher level and down would come the tree in the expected place. If during the axing there should be some doubt about this expectancy then a degree of tilt could be maintained using wedges. This became even more important if the tree was leaning at an angle in the first place. Cutting close to the ground looks like being a tradition that developed after the Saxons arrived, since in Germany they cut much higher (and in America).

Wedges really came into their own whenever saws were used. They were driven in behind the saw to prevent the tree sitting back on the blade and pinching it. Of course these wedges trapped the blade in the heart of the tree, so the handles of felling saws were made detachable, and then the blade could be withdrawn sideways. For all its different qualities of strength, Hornbeam wood is best suited for these wedges. Being harder than practically any other tree it was used against meant it was the tree, not the wedge, which yielded. It's not entirely ideal though, for the wedge is slow to make. As the wood won't split you have to stop and saw it into shape. Therefore, many woodsmen resorted to a piece of very well seasoned heartwood from an Oak. That will cleave. It's just as good for doing the job and for most of the country, outside the range of the Hornbeam, there was no option.

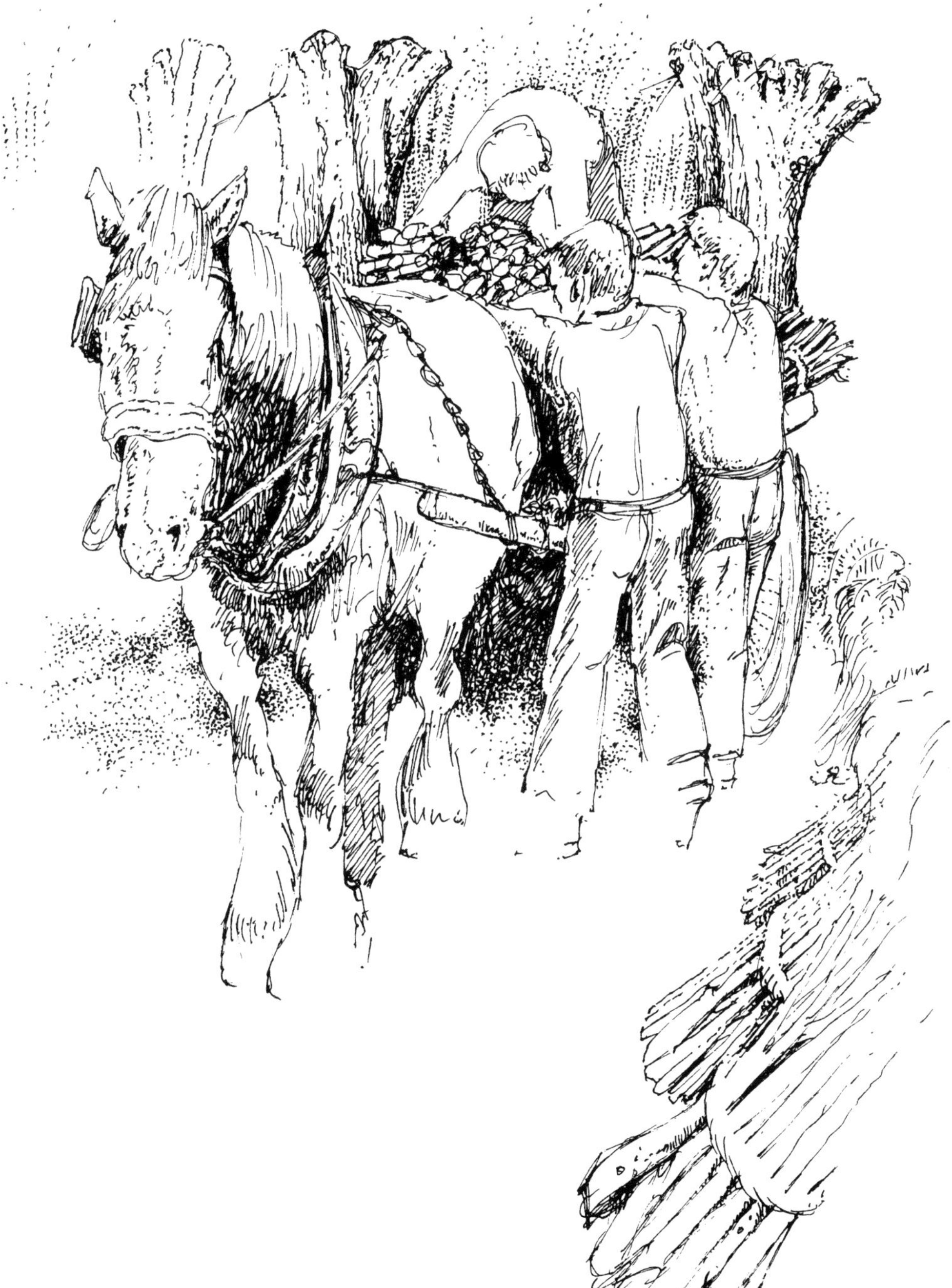

Once the tree is down and the trunk cleaned of branches (known as *snedding* in many regions) the wedges work miracles. As you watch the woodsmen tapping a line of them into the length of the trunk you are left with no conviction that these will split the tree in half – but they do! Unbelievably, the sharp edges of the wedges *are* sharp enough to penetrate an Oak. Very soon the rending noise tells you the top layer is being forced free of the lower. Do this time and again and you can soon reduce a tree trunk to a stack of planks. If they're too wide, they can be split lengthways.

Traditionally, all this working was relatively quiet. Woodsmen didn't like the clang, clang, clang of metal against metal, so not only were the old wedges made of wood but so too were the sledge-hammers. These *beetles* or *mauls* had Ash handles and Hornbeam heads – really big heads, compared with a modern sledge-hammer. An apprentice had to be really inept to miss the wedge with one of those! Once saw benches arrived in the woods then Hornbeam was used sometimes for the *bushes* or bearings that carried the rotating spindle.

There's a Hornbeam wedge, beautiful to handle, in the collections at Kew. At the butt end it's 4cm thick and 7cm wide, tapering for 27cm to its front edge, and that is 2cm narrower than the butt end. It came from France, from Noyen, Oise. It's intended purpose is unknown but it's so finely finished it is unlikely to have been a woodsman's.

Among the Hornbeams themselves you might have found, in the past, people who worked for the barrel-makers or coopers (from the Latin *cupa* for cask). The tree has been used for both the staves (wooden slats that make up the body) and the hoops (wooden rings that hold the staves). In particular, Hornbeam gets recorded for fish barrels and specifically for packed herrings (which were a very important item in the medieval diet). In this case, Hornbeam was used for *dry* or *slack* coopering, i.e. for barrels that did not have to be absolutely water-tight. This makes sense, as the waterproof or *wet* coopering relied upon the way the staves were split, with wedges, which of course wouldn't happen with Hornbeam. Even so, it must have been a determined workshop that sawed all the Hornbeam staves by hand. Perhaps then, we should think more in terms of *white* coopering, which was the making of smaller casks for dairy and household uses – the whiteness of the timber being well suited. Anyone reading further on the subject of coopering should bear in mind that most descriptions in print are for *wet* coopering with Oak; we have our doubts that Hornbeam would have responded in the same way to some of the procedures.

Whereas the cooper worked from premises, the hooper was a coppice worker. He cut rods from coppiced stools to loop round and fix into hoops, which were used primarily by the coopers. There were other uses though, ranging from sieve and seed-lip rims to retaining hoops amid the rigging of sailing craft. The rods were heated over a fire until pliable and then forced into curvature, using a wooden horse and then finally curved round a spoked device, that also standardised them, until the ends could be nailed. Six of them made a *coil* and the coils were sold in dozens. It was a very important occupation in the Hornbeam district although it's a little surprising to learn that the rods responded sufficiently well to heat bending to be so employed.

Barrels and casks were the universal containers, for both wet and dry goods, on land and at sea, for hundreds of years, and well into the 20th century. Their importance should not be underestimated. The cooper was originally a craftsman of high status.

It would have been rare to see men out in the woods scanning the trees in search of a specimen that would fulfil some special need. Perhaps, just occasionally they'd have to search for a central post for a windmill. Otherwise it's the people involved with cutting the coppices and pollards for fuel, whether firewood or charcoal, who need to be imagined - hard at work before the poles became too unmanageable.

******

THE WOODWORKER

The village carpenter, traditionally, could turn his hand to whatever was needed – from windmills to egg cups. Part of his working life was likely to be spent at the lathe and so this chapter should be read in conjunction with that titled *The Turner*. They've been separated to highlight the importance of the turners' screws.

Carpenters' tools were often of Hornbeam because it was so hard wearing and doesn't put splinters into his hands. Handles are worth a close inspection, especially chisels, because Hornbeam will resist splitting when struck with a mallet. Look at planes too. Sometimes you can find one with a sole (the working surface with the blade mouth) that is not made from one single piece but has been 'boxed' up. There's the main central sole, usually of Beech which is best for the job, and an outer narrow frame of Hornbeam. Invariably this has been beautifully dovetailed together; a work of art in itself, as beautiful as some of the furnishings it made. The reasoning behind this double structure is to ensure an even wear. The outer Hornbeam is more resistant to abrasion than the Beech and so the latter prolongs the life of the sole. Although these tools can be found in Britain, the collectors of treen and old tools report that as far as they know we never *made* them here. Germany is the usual source cited. In the collections at Kew is a beautiful little plane (18.5cm x 6cm; thickness 6.5cm) made entirely from Hornbeam and bearing a Paris label.

To see this partnership between Beech and Hornbeam working in reverse, have a look at traditional butchers' chopping blocks, on top of the counter. Here you can find the Hornbeam block has been framed in Beech. Thus the frame will abrade faster than the central block, leaving the latter proud. That's just what the butcher wants. He doesn't want a hollow block. Apart from its hard-wearing qualities, Hornbeam has other characteristics suited to this job – it doesn't put splinters into the food and it doesn't release contaminants such as smell, taste or dye. For the same reasons Elm was chosen for the main chopping block that people still remember in the middle of the shop floor. These stood about a metre high and half a metre square. Like Hornbeam, Elm is resistant to splitting, if it's a piece with well-twisted grain, and was chosen for this use because it was available in large blocks.

Mallets have been made in a wide range of styles to suit various tasks, not just the squared block on a handle that is associated with woodworkers today. There's a French one in the Kew collections. It's 32cm long, of which 15cm is taken up by the head which is otherwise 14cm x 14.5cm. Sometimes they are called *dressers*, as in the case for plumbers, who needed a wooden head rather than a metal hammerhead which would damage their lead. Again, there's a French one at Kew, from Noyon, Oise, and date labelled 1881. It has a round head, 6.5cm diameter on a 33cm handle. Another French round one, of unknown use, labelled Paris 1881, has a much larger head at 11cm and a shorter handle at 25cm. Totally different in design are a pair of French zinc-beaters' mallets (34cm long).

Brushes will serve to turn us away from the general practitioner to the specialist. By the end of the Victorian era brushes were being made for every conceivable use. It's a demanding job for the woodwork. Not only has it got to withstand rough treatment but, most importantly, it must be capable of being close drilled with all those little holes to take the bunches of bristles. Most woods crack up under such treatment. The common yard broom has a massive wooden block, partly for weight, but also to withstand the drilling. Such block heads are unsuitable for domestic usage as they obstruct the brush from confined spaces. The engineering qualities of Hornbeam do permit this close drilling, in just the same way as exploited for harpsichord jacks.

At Kew a French scrubbing brush (from Noyon, Oise, 1881) shows this well. It's been drilled so closely it defeated the maker; a couple of holes converge upon each other! That's where they are more concentrated, towards the rounded front end. The square back end has six holes drilled parallel with the surface so that they join up with the first row drilled in at right angles and still the wood is sound. Overall it's 20cm x 7cm and is of the design that has a handle, humping over the back. It's pinned into place. Another Kew brush, from the same source, is labelled a 'dandy brush', i.e. for cleaning horses. When these came into being in 1841 they were normally of whalebone[71] but as whales became scarcer so other materials became important. This one has the holes drilled right through. It's only 29 x 7cm and yet tolerates five rows of holes, the outer two being smaller than the inner three, with the longest central row comprising 20 holes. Still the wood is sound.

Furniture workshops would be another specialist category here but rarely has Hornbeam been used. The irregularity of its growth produces much timber that is 'cross-grained' making it wonderfully strong but very difficult for the joiner and cabinet-maker to work. It was, therefore, quite a surprise at Kew to find a plastic bag catalogued as "bag of four turned items including chair parts; British."

---

[71] *Oxford English Dictionary*

BIBLIOGRAPHY

Allaby, Michael; *The Woodland Trust Book of British Woodlands*; David & Charles, 1986.
Arnold, James; *Farm Waggons and Carts*; David and Charles; 1977.
Beeton, Mrs; *The Beeton Book of Garden Management*; fasc. Omega Books; 1985.
Bellamy, David; *Woodland Walks*; Hamlyn; 1992.
Birdsall, Derek and Cipolla, Carlo M.; *The Technology of Man*; Penshurst Press; 1980.
Boalch, D.; *Makers of the Harpsichord and Clavichord 1440-1840*; Oxford Clarendon Press; 1974.
Brace, H. W.; *History of Seed Crushing in Great Britain*; Land Books; 1960
Brimble, L.; *Trees in Britain*; MacMillan; 1948.
Clarke, Ethne and Wright, George; *English Topiary Gardens*; Weidenfeld & Nicholson;1998.
Cobbett, William; *The English Gardener*; 1829; repr. Bloomsbury Garden Classics; 1996.
Edlin, Herbert; *Woodland Crafts in Britain*; Country Book Club ed. 1974.
Ellis, Jeff.; *The Clubmaker's Art*; Zephyr; 1997.
Encyclopaedia. Britannica; 15th ed.; 1997.
Evelyn, John; *Silva: or a Discourse of Forest Trees*; 5th ed. 1729.
French, R. K.; *The History and Virtues of Cyder*; Robert Hale; 1982.
Fussell, G. E.; *The English Countryman*; Bloomsbury Bks. Ed.1985.
The Farmers' Tools; Bloomsbury Bks ed.1985.
Godwin, Harry; *History of the British Flora*; 2nd ed. CUP; 1975.
Grew, Frances and Deneergard, Margretha; *Shoes and Pattens (Medieval Finds from Excavations in London)*; HMSO.
Hammond, P. W.; *Food and Feast in Medieval England*; Sutton Publishing; 1993.
Henderson, Ian T. and Stirk, David I.; *Golf in the Making*; Arnold; 1982.
Howkins, Chris.; *Trees, Herbs and Charcoal Burners*; Chris Howkins; 1994.
Hubbard, Frank; *Three Centuries of Harpsichord Making*; Harvard; 1965.
Hulme, F. Edward, *Wild Fruits of the Country-side*; Hutchinson, 1902.
Jekyll, Gertrude; *Old West Surrey*; Longmans; 1904.
Johnson, C. P.; *The Useful Plants of Great Britain*; Hardwicke, 1862.
Jolly, Karen; *Popular Religion in Late Saxon England – Elf Charms in Context*; Univ. of N. Carolina Press; 1996.
Lee, Lawrence., Seddon, George, and Stephens, Francis; *Stained Glass*; Mitchel Beazley; 1976.
Lewington, Anna; *Plants for People*; The Natural History Museum; 1990.
Lloyd, Christopher;*The Cottage Garden*; Dorling Kindersley; 1990.
Lovett, Maurice; *Brewing and Breweries*; Shire; 1981.

Mabey, Richard; *Flora Britannica*; Sinclair-Stevenson; 1996.
Miller, Christie; *The Hornbeam in Britain*; J. of Ecology; Vol.XII; No.1; 1924.
Milner, J. Edward; *The Tree Book*; Collins and Brown; 1992.
Moran, James; *Printing Presses: A History and Development from the Fifteenth Century to Modern Times*; Faber; 1973.
Pearson, F. G. O. and Webster, Constance; *Timbers Used in the Musical Instruments Industry*; Forest Products Research Laboratory, for Ministry of Technology, 1956.
Pollock, Michael, *The Performance of the Wooden Printing Press*; Univ. of Chicago Press; 1972.
Quinion, Michael; *Cidermaking*; Shire; 1982.
Rackham, Oliver; *History of the Countryside*; Dent; 1986.
Rose, Walter; *The Village Carpenter*; CUP; 1937.
Russell, Raymond; *The Harpsichord and Clavichord*; Faber; 1959.
Seymour, John; *The National Trust Book of Forgotten Household Crafts*; Dorling Kindersley; 1987.
Sparkes, Ivan; *Woodland Craftsmen*; Shire; 1977.
Sim, Alison; *Food and Feast in Tudor England*; Sutton Publishing; 1997.
Sturt, George; *The Wheelwright's Shop*; 1923 (1963 ed. used).
Tabor, Raymond; *Traditional Woodland Crafts*; Batsford; 1994.
Trow-Smith, Robert; *A History of British Livestock Husbandry*; Routledge and Keegan Paul; 2 vols. 1955.
Urquhart, Judy; *Animals on the Farm: Their History from the Earliest Times to the Present Day*; MacDonald; 1983.
Whitlock, Ralph; *The English Farm*; Dent; 1983.
Wilks, J. H.; *Trees of the British Isles, in History and Legend*; Frederick Muller; 1972.
Worlidge, J; *Vinetum Britannicum or a Treatise of Cider...*; 1676.
Young, Geoffrey; *Traditional British Crafts*; Marshall Cavendish; 1989.

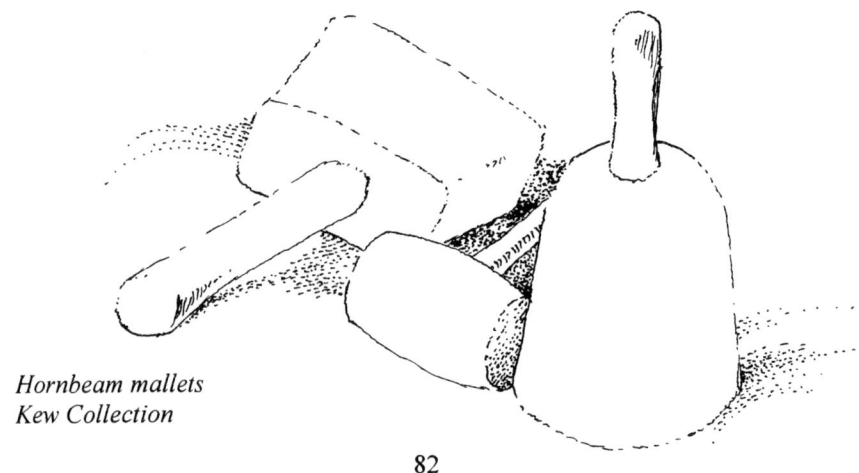

Hornbeam mallets
Kew Collection

CHECKLIST OF DOCUMENTED USES FOUND TO DATE

Arrows
Axle arms
Axle beds
Balls
Beetle heads
Billiard cues
Boot trees
Bowls, playing
Brush backs
Bushes, machine
Butchers' chopping blocks
Chairs, turned components
Charcoal
Chess men
Clubs, woodsmen's
Cogs and gear teeth, in mills
Dominoes
Draughts men
Dressers, plumbers'
Dye, yellow
Electric switch handles
Fence rails
Firewood and firelighters
Floors, particularly threshing
Golf clubs
Handles, tool
Harpsichords
Hoops
Hop poles
Lasts
Mallets
Mauls
Pianos
Plane stocks
Post mills

Pulleys
Pulley pins
Ramrods for guns
Scrabble tiles
Screws
Skittles and balls
Staves, coopers'
Steles
Turned items
Veneers as wallpaper
Walking sticks
Wedges
Yokes, ox

GENERAL INDEX

Ascham, Roger 4
Alder 8, 27
Alleys 21
America, North 10, 41, 51, 74
Apple wood, 34, 35, 41, 46, 53
Apples, cider 61-3
Ash 15, 47, 50, 54, 55, 56, 76
Asia Minor 10
Avenues 21
Axles 70-3

Bagpipes 46
Balata 54
Balls, wooden 49
Barrels 76-8
Bedford Park 24
Beech 8, 11, 12, 15, 23, 31, 34, 39, 53, 71, 78, 79; Dawyck 25
Beetles 76
Beeton, Mrs 23
Billiards 49-50
Birch 8, 15-6, 57
Blackthorn 53, 56
Blackwood, African 46
Boloeil, Belgium 22
Bowls, playing 50-2
Box 14, 15, 16, 40
Bread 31-2
Brewing 27
Brown, Capability 22
Brush backs 79-80
Bushes, sawbench 76
Butchers' blocks 79

Caesar, Julius 11
Carpinus spp. and cvs. 10, 13
Caucasus 10
Caxton, William 61
Chairs 80
Characteristics of tree 8

Charcoal 27
Cherry 24, 53, 57
Chess 54
Chestnut, Horse 24
Chilterns 27
Cider presses 61-3
Clavichords 46
Cobbett, William 23
Conifers 23
Cobblers 17
Coopering 76-7
Coppicing 11, 13-4, 25
Cordwainers 18
Cotswolds 47, 73
Cristofori, B. 42
Croydon 27

Density of wood 14
Devon 48, 62, 63
Dogwood 53
Dolmetsch family 45-6
Dominoes 54
Drake, Sir Francis 52
Draughts 54
Dressers, tool 79
Drums 46

Ebony 41, 50
Elms 34, 55, 73, 79
Ely Cathedral 37
Enfield Chase 27
Epping Forest 27, 29
Essex 27, 28, 29
Etiquette, table 63-5
Evelyn, John 17, 21, 48, 68, 69

Felling 74-7
Flails 55, 56
Flax 65, 66
Floatation 15, 16

Folklore 6
Fruits 11
Fuel 25-31, 49, 78
Fungi 5
Furniture 80

Garden City style 24
Garden use 21-5
Glass industry 27, 52
Gloucestershire 52, 71, 73
Golf 52-4
Grazing 11
Greece 10
Gunpowder 27
Gutenberg, Johan 59-61
Gwent 10, 33

Hainault Forest 27, 29
Hampton Court 21
Handles, tool 78
Harpsichords 40, 44-5
Harvests, corn 31
Haslemere 45
Hawfinch 8
Hawthorn 53, 56
Hazel 8, 27
Hedging 21
Hemp 65, 66
Hertfordshire 11, 27, 73
Hickory 54
Hidcote Manor 24
Holly 16, 23, 46, 53
Hoopers 13, 77-8
Horses 47, 48
Howard, Ebenezer 24
Hubs 71, 72, 73-4
Hurley, Hugh 37

Iron industry 27
Italy 10

Jekyll, Gertrude 23, 24, 56-7
Johnson, C. P. 17

Johnston, Lawrence 24

Kent 27, 73
Keys and keyboards 40
Kingston-upon-Thames 27

Labyrinths 21
Lambarde, Giles 67
Lasts 17
Lewes 39
Lighting 13, 65, 67, 69
Lignum vitae 52
Lincolnshire 73
Linen presses 63-5
Linnaues, Carl 12
Linseed oil 65
Lloyd, Christopher 23
London 24, 25, 61
Lopping Hall 28, 30
Loughton 28, 29
Luther, Martin 50

Mallets 79
Management, woodland 13
Maples 11, 43, 44, 50
Mauls 76
Mazes 21
Medhurst, George 39
Meikle, Andrew 57
Millers 31
Musicians 40-6
Mustards 65

Names, English 12-3, 31
Naves 73
Napkins 65
Nine pins 51
Noettes, Lefevre des, 47
Northamptonshire 19, 73

Oak 10, 11, 15, 16, 27, 34, 38, 41, 55, 71, 74, 76, 77
Oils, edible 65

Oil seed presses 65-8
Orthotics 19
Outwood 36, 38, 39
Oxen 46-8
Oxfordshire 18, 73

Paint 69
Parks 21
Pear wood 14, 15, 34, 35, 41, 53
Persimmon 54
Pianos 40, 42
Pimps 31
Plane, London, tree 24
Plane, tool 78
Pliny 12
Ploughman 46-8
Plum wood 53
Pollarding 11, 13-14, 25, 26
Pollen 11
Poplars 25
Prehistory 11
Preservation of wood 17
Presses 59-69
Printing press 59-61
Privet 23

Ramin 50
Range of tree 10
Rape 65-8
Rosewood 50

Sapele 43
Saspach, Conrad 60
Scotland 53, 54, 56
Scrabble 54
Screws 58
Seasoning 17
Serviette rings 57
Shakespeare, William 49
Shipley 38, 39
Shipping 5, 62
Shoe-making 17
Skenfrith 33

Skittles 50-2
Soap 65
Somerset 10
Spalting 17
Specific gravity 15
Sports and games 49-54
Steles 4
Storrs, John, workshop 40
Sunderland 10
Surrey 36, 68, 71, 73
Sussex 38, 39, 48, 73
Sycamore 16, 25, 55

Table cloths 64
Textile industry 67
Thorn trees 23
Threshing 55-7
Trees, shoe 19
Tulip tree 16, 45
Turning, wood 57-8

Uranium 5

Varnish 69
Veneers 5
Vetruvius 12

Walnut oil 68
Wash, the 10
Watermills 32-5
Weald 27
Wedges 75-6
Wheelwrights 70-4
Whiteness of wood 16
Wiltshire 47
Windmills 13, 36-9, 78
Woodsman 74-8
Woodworker 78-80

Yew 23, 53
Yokes, ox 46-8